A necessity for every golfer, *The Rules of Golf in Plain English* is the first word-by-word translation of the Rules of Golf and is published with the permission of the United States Golf Association.

"Clear, useful, and very authoritative. . . . *The Rules of Golf in Plain English* is a valuable tool for anyone with an interest in the Rules of Golf. It is a good and interesting read, regardless of whether the reader is an expert or a novice in interpreting and applying the Rules."
David Fay, *former executive director, United States Golf Association*

THE RULES OF **GOLF** IN PLAIN ENGLISH

THE RULES OF GO

LF
IN PLAIN ENGLISH
FOURTH EDITION

Jeffrey S. Kuhn & Bryan A. Garner

THE UNIVERSITY OF CHICAGO PRESS
CHICAGO AND LONDON

Excerpts from *The Rules of Golf* and *Decisions on the Rules of Golf* are reprinted from *The Rules of Golf* 2015–2016 and *Decisions on the Rules of Golf* 2015–2016, © 2016 United States Golf Association, with permission. All rights reserved.

This book is a summary of some of *The Rules of Golf* and *Decisions on the Rules of Golf* as interpreted by the authors. It does not carry the official approval of the USGA, which does not therefore warrant the accuracy of the authors' interpretation. Readers should refer to the full text of the *Rules* and *Decisions* as published in the official publications, *The Rules of Golf* and *Decisions on the Rules of Golf*, which are published by the USGA/R&A.

The University of Chicago Press, Chicago 60637
The University of Chicago Press, Ltd., London
© 2004, 2008, 2012, 2016 by Jeffrey S. Kuhn and Bryan A. Garner
All rights reserved. Published 2016.
Printed in the United States of America

25 24 23 22 21 20 19 18 17 16   1 2 3 4 5

ISBN-13: 978-0-226-37145-0 (paper)
ISBN-13: 978-0-226-37159-7 (e-book)
DOI: 10.7208/chicago/9780226371597.001.0001

Library of Congress Cataloging-in-Publication Data

Names: Kuhn, Jeffrey S., author. | Garner, Bryan A., author.
Title: The rules of golf in plain English.
Description: Fourth edition / Jeffrey S. Kuhn & Bryan A. Garner | Chicago ; London : The University of Chicago Press, 2016. | Includes index.
Identifiers: LCCN 2015049563 | ISBN 9780226371450 (pbk. : alk. paper) | ISBN 9780226371597 (e-book)
Subjects: LCSH: Golf—Rules.
Classification: LCC GV971 .K85 2016 | DDC 796.352/3—dc23 LC record available at http://lccn.loc.gov/2015049563

♾ This paper meets the requirements of ANSI/NISO Z39.48-1992 (Permanence of Paper).

The cry for simplification of the Rules of Golf is a stock-in-trade of the journalist during the winter months. Countless words on the subject have been poured out to an ever-tolerant public, but still the long-sought simplification does not come.

— Henry Longhurst, 1937

CONTENTS

Preface *xvii*

RULE 1 THE GAME
- 1.1 Description *1*
- 1.2 Primary Rules *1*
- 1.3 No Agreement to Ignore Rules *2*
- 1.4 Issues Not Covered by Rules *2*

RULE 2 MATCH PLAY
- 2.1 Scoring and Winning the Match *3*
- 2.2 Penalties *3*
- 2.3 Concession *4*
- 2.4 Claims *4*
- 2.5 Information About Strokes Taken *5*

RULE 3 STROKE PLAY
- 3.1 Scoring *7*
- 3.2 Penalties *7*
- 3.3 Failing to Hole Out *7*
- 3.4 Player's Doubt About Procedures *7*

RULE 4 CLUBS
- 4.1 Original Design and Changes *10*
- 4.2 Damaged Clubs: Allowable Repair and Replacement *11*
- 4.3 Fourteen-Club Maximum *12*

RULE 5 THE BALL
- 5.1 General *14*
- 5.2 Foreign-Material Restriction *14*
- 5.3 Damaged Ball *14*
- 5.4 Broken Ball *15*

RULE 6 THE PLAYER'S RESPONSIBILITIES
- 6.1 Rules *16*
- 6.2 Handicap *16*
- 6.3 Starting Time and Groups *16*
- 6.4 Caddie *17*
- 6.5 Ball *18*
- 6.6 Scoring in Stroke Play *18*
- 6.7 Undue Delay and Slow Play *19*
- 6.8 Stopping Play and Resuming Play *20*

RULE 7 PRACTICE
- 7.1 Before and Between Rounds *23*
- 7.2 Restrictions During Round *24*
- 7.3 During Suspended Play *24*

RULE 8 ADVICE AND INDICATING LINE OF PLAY
- 8.1 Advice Restrictions *25*
- 8.2 Indicating Line of Play *25*
- 8.3 Advice Exception for Team Competitions *26*
- 8.4 Penalty *27*

RULE 9 INFORMATION ABOUT STROKES TAKEN [DELETED AND INCORPORATED INTO RULES 3.1(B) AND 2.5]

RULE 10 ORDER OF PLAY
- 10.1 Match Play *28*
- 10.2 Stroke Play *29*
- 10.3 Provisional Ball or Second Ball from Teeing Ground *30*

RULE 11 TEEING GROUND
- 11.1 Teeing the Ball *30*
- 11.2 Tee-Markers *31*
- 11.3 Ball Falling off Tee *31*

11.4	Playing from Outside Teeing Ground 31
11.5	Playing from Wrong Teeing Ground 32

RULE 12   SEARCHING FOR AND IDENTIFYING BALL

12.1	Searching for Ball and Seeing Ball 32
12.2	Identifying Ball 34

RULE 13   PLAYING THE BALL AS IT LIES

13.1	General 36
13.2	Improving Lie, Stance, or Swing, or Line of Play Through the Green 36
13.3	Building Stance 37
13.4	Ball in Hazard 37
13.5	Penalty 38

RULE 14   STRIKING THE BALL; ARTIFICIAL DEVICES

14.1	Strike with Clubhead Only 39
14.2	Anchoring the Club Is Not Allowed 39
14.3	No Assistance 39
14.4	Artificial Devices, Unusual Equipment, and Abnormal Use of Equipment 39
14.5	Multiple Strikes 40
14.6	Playing a Moving Ball 40
14.7	Ball Moving in Water in a Water Hazard 41

RULE 15   SUBSTITUTED BALL; WRONG BALL

15.1	General Rule for Substituted Ball 42
15.2	Wrong Ball in Match Play 43
15.3	Wrong Ball in Stroke Play 43

RULE 16   THE PUTTING GREEN

16.1	General 44
16.2	Ball Overhanging Hole 46

RULE 17   THE FLAGSTICK

17.1	Flagstick Attended, Held Up, or Removed 47

17.2	Unauthorized Attendance 47
17.3	Ball Striking Flagstick or Attendant 48
17.4	Ball Resting Against Flagstick 48

RULE 18 MOVEMENT OF BALL AT REST

18.1	Ball Moved by an Outside Agency 49
18.2	Ball Moved by Player, Partner, Caddie, or Equipment 50
18.3	Ball Moved by Opponent, Caddie, or Equipment in Match Play 51
18.4	Ball Moved by a Fellow-Competitor, Caddie, or Equipment in Stroke Play 51
18.5	Ball Moved by Another Ball 51
18.6	Ball Moved in Measuring 51
18.7	Procedures and Penalties 52

RULE 19 MOVING BALL DEFLECTED OR STOPPED

19.1	By Outside Agency 53
19.2	By Player, Partner, Caddie, or Equipment 54
19.3	By Opponent, Caddie, or Equipment in Match Play 54
19.4	By Fellow-Competitor, Caddie, or Equipment in Stroke Play 55
19.5	By Another Ball 55
19.6	Penalty 56

RULE 20 PROCEDURES FOR LIFTING, DROPPING, AND PLACING; PLAYING FROM WRONG PLACE

20.1	Marking and Lifting the Ball 57
20.2	Dropping and Re-Dropping the Ball 58
20.3	Placing or Returning the Ball 60
20.4	When Ball Is In Play 62
20.5	Playing Next Stroke from Where Previous Stroke Played 62

20.6	Lifting Ball Incorrectly Substituted, Dropped, or Placed 63
20.7	Playing from Wrong Place 63

RULE 21 CLEANING YOUR BALL
- 21.1 General Rule 65
- 21.2 Penalty and Procedures 65
- 21.3 Penalty Limits 66

RULE 22 BALL INTERFERING WITH OR ASSISTING PLAY
- 22.1 General Rule 66
- 22.2 Exceptions 66
- 22.3 No Cleaning 67
- 22.4 Penalties 67

RULE 23 LOOSE IMPEDIMENTS
- 23.1 General Rule 67
- 23.2 Ball Moving After a Loose Impediment Is Touched 68
- 23.3 Exception 68
- 23.4 Penalty 68

RULE 24 INTERFERENCE AND RELIEF FROM OBSTRUCTIONS
- 24.1 Movable Obstructions 69
- 24.2 Immovable Obstructions 70
- 24.3 Ball Not Found in an Obstruction 72

RULE 25 INTERFERENCE AND RELIEF FROM ABNORMAL GROUND CONDITIONS, EMBEDDED BALL, OR WRONG PUTTING GREEN
- 25.1 Abnormal Ground Condition 74
- 25.2 Ball Not Found in Abnormal Ground Condition 76
- 25.3 Embedded Ball 77

	25.4	Wrong Putting Green 78
	25.5	Penalty 78
RULE 26		**WATER HAZARDS**
	26.1	Ball in a Water Hazard 79
	26.2	Ball Played from Within a Water Hazard 80
RULE 27		**BALL LOST OR OUT OF BOUNDS; PROVISIONAL BALL**
	27.1	Ball Lost or Out of Bounds 82
	27.2	Provisional Ball 83
RULE 28		**UNPLAYABLE BALL**
	28.1	General Rule and Options 85
	28.2	Bunker Restriction 86
	28.3	Penalty 86
RULE 29		**THREESOMES AND FOURSOMES**
	29.1	General Format 87
	29.2	Incorrect Order in Match Play 87
	29.3	Incorrect Order in Stroke Play 87
RULE 30		**THREE-BALL, BEST-BALL, AND FOUR-BALL MATCH PLAY**
	30.1	General 88
	30.2	Three-Ball Match Play 88
	30.3	Best-Ball and Four-Ball Match Play 89
RULE 31		**FOUR-BALL STROKE PLAY**
	31.1	General Format 91
	31.2	Representing a Side 91
	31.3	Scoring 92
	31.4	Order of Play 92
	31.5	Wrong Ball 92
	31.6	Side Penalized 92
	31.7	Disqualification Penalties 92
	31.8	Effect of Other Penalties 94

RULE 32 BOGEY, PAR, AND STABLEFORD COMPETITIONS

- 32.1 Definition and Conditions *94*
- 32.2 Disqualification Penalties *97*

RULE 33 THE COMMITTEE

- 33.1 Authority and Restrictions *99*
- 33.2 Course Responsibilities *99*
- 33.3 Starting Times and Groups *100*
- 33.4 Handicap Stroke Table *101*
- 33.5 Decision for Ties *101*
- 33.6 Scorecard Responsibilities *101*

RULE 34 DISPUTES AND DECISIONS

- 34.1 Time Limits for Claims and Penalties *102*
- 34.2 Referee's Decision *104*
- 34.3 Committee's Decision and Appeal *104*

RULE 35 DEFINITIONS

- 35.1 Abnormal Ground Condition *105*
- 35.2 Addressing the Ball *105*
- 35.3 Advice *105*
- 35.4 Ball in Play *105*
- 35.5 Ball Unfit for Play *106*
- 35.6 Bunker *106*
- 35.7 Caddie *107*
- 35.8 Casual Water *107*
- 35.9 Closely Mown Area *107*
- 35.10 Club Unfit for Play *108*
- 35.11 Committee *108*
- 35.12 Competitor *108*
- 35.13 Course *108*
- 35.14 Equipment *108*
- 35.15 Flagstick *109*
- 35.16 Forecaddie *109*
- 35.17 Forms of Match Play *109*

35.18	Forms of Stroke Play	110
35.19	Ground Under Repair	110
35.20	Handicap	111
35.21	Hazard	111
35.22	Hole	111
35.23	Hole Out	112
35.24	Honor	112
35.25	Lateral Water Hazard	112
35.26	Line of Play	113
35.27	Line of Putt	113
35.28	Loose Impediment	113
35.29	Lost Ball	113
35.30	Move	114
35.31	Nearest Point of Relief	114
35.32	Observer	115
35.33	Obstruction	115
35.34	Opponent	115
35.35	Out of Bounds	115
35.36	Outside Agency	116
35.37	Partner	116
35.38	Penalty Stroke	117
35.39	Provisional Ball	117
35.40	Putting Green	117
35.41	Referee	117
35.42	Rule	117
35.43	Scorer	118
35.44	Side	118
35.45	Stance	118
35.46	Stipulated Round	118
35.47	Stroke	118
35.48	Substituted Ball	118
35.49	Tee	119
35.50	Teeing Ground	119
35.51	Through the Green	119

35.52 Water Hazard *119*
35.53 Wrong Ball *120*
35.54 Wrong Putting Green *120*

Appendix 1. Penalty Summary Chart *121*
Appendix 2. Golf Etiquette *125*

Index *129*

PREFACE

This book doesn't *explain* the Rules of Golf. Many other books have done that, with varying degrees of success. Instead, it *translates* them, faithfully, into plain English. It makes them readily accessible to a wide readership — from seasoned players to beginners, not to mention fans of the game. It doesn't "dumb down" the rules. Not at all. Rather, it employs Albert Einstein's principle about expressing ideas as simply as possible without oversimplifying them.

A LITTLE HISTORY OF THE RULES

The Rules of Golf trace their lineage to 1744, when the golfers of Leith, Scotland, drew up thirteen rules of play comprising just 338 words (printable in half a page). Some of these original rules are familiar to modern golfers: "If you should lose your ball . . . you are to go back to the spot where you struck last, and drop another ball, and allow your adversary a stroke for the misfortune." In today's informal nomenclature, we call this "stroke and distance."

By 1812, the code posted by the St. Andrews Society of Golfers had grown to seventeen rules, still printable in less than a page, comprising 541 words. The lost-ball rule (like all the others) lost the second-person *you*, which was replaced by the third-person *player*. Although the 1812 rule more closely resembles the modern rule, the phrasing still seems quaint: "If a ball is lost, the stroke goes for nothing, the player returns to the spot whence the ball was struck, tees it, and loses a stroke." And in this 1812 code, the famous phrase *loose impediments* made its debut: "All loose impediments of whatever kind may be removed upon the putting green."

The rules evolved. In 1899, the Royal and Ancient Golf Club of St. Andrews (R&A) issued its first official code, which underwent periodic revisions. In 1921, the "provisional ball" was added to speed play. In 1922, golf balls were first required to be uniform in weight and size. In 1939, the maximum number of clubs was set at 14.

Meanwhile, the United States Golf Association (USGA) had taken root in 1894, and gradually it diverged from the R&A on various points, from the size of the golf ball to the out-of-bounds rule to the penalty for an unplayable lie. The first chair of the USGA Committee on Rules suggested that the American adaptations made golf "more adaptable to American links."

Then, in 1952, the rules became uniform worldwide as the USGA and the R&A joined forces to issue a single rulebook. Among other changes, they abolished the stymie — at the insistence of the Americans — and agreed that the scorecard must be countersigned by the competitor.

Decade by decade, the rulebook grew. By 1970, it was 75 pages comprising about 18,000 words. By 2003, it was 132 pages, in smaller type, comprising nearly 40,000 words. Words and pages have proliferated to deal with the endless variety of issues that the game of golf continually raises. Anyone who doubts the complexity of these issues should take a look at *Decisions on the Rules of Golf,* the 600-page question-and-answer encyclopedia of golf rulings intended as a companion volume to the Rules of Golf.

Over several generations, many hands the world over have contributed to the Rules of Golf. As with any body of rules that have evolved over time, stylistic inconsistencies have crept in. The style is sometimes wooden, legalistic, and opaque.

Ordinary golfers have learned not to expect much enlightenment when reading through the rules. This is particularly troublesome in a sport that has traditionally prided itself on the history of players' calling penalties on themselves. How ironic that one of the game's traditions is hindered by a cumbersome code.

Believing that ordinary golfers should reasonably expect to understand the rules that govern their play, we've rewritten the rules to maximize readability.

HOW THIS PROJECT CAME ABOUT

We're both golfers, and we're both lawyers. One of us (Garner) has spent many years training lawyers and judges to write in plain English. He has written many books on the subject, such as *Legal Writing in Plain English* (2001). Over the past twenty-five years, he has taught more than 3,500 seminars on the subject. The other (Kuhn) was a participant in one of those seminars. More important, he has devoted himself for over two decades to attending USGA rules seminars and officiating at many USGA championships; he has been at the center of some particularly difficult rulings in major events.

Upon learning of Garner's experience in revising the Federal Rules of Appellate Procedure and other sets of state and federal rules, Kuhn approached Garner during a break in a legal-drafting seminar in March 1999. He said: "What we should really work on is the Rules of Golf."

After talking it over, the two of us agreed to embark on the project. We worked through draft after draft — ten in all. We simplified wordings, added headings and subheadings throughout, improved the numbering system, adopted the second-person *you* (not even knowing, at the time, about the 1744 precedent for this convention), eliminated sexist wordings, added contractions where they seemed natural, made every subsection citable, and rearranged a few provisions to make the rules read more logically. We did all the things that good legislative drafters do to make their work accessible to as many people as possible.

We've had some excellent help with this project. Jeff Kuhn's legal assistant, Andrea Hecht, organized materials, typed the manuscript, and entered corrections countless times — always with great skill. Jamie Conkling, a PGA Tour official, reviewed our early drafts to ensure that we were faithful to the rules. Jeff Hall, Bernie Loehr, John Van der Borght, and Rob Ockenfuss of the USGA helped us incorporate official 2004, 2008, 2012, and 2016 rules changes into our translation.

Jeff Newman and Tiger Jackson of LawProse Inc., expertly proofread the manuscript. Linda J. Halvorson of the University of Chicago Press expedited the book's approval and publication.

The USGA generously gave its permission for us to publish this translation. We dedicate this book to golfers everywhere. It's for the good of the game.

Bryan A. Garner
Jeffrey S. Kuhn

RULE 1. The Game

1.0 DEFINED TERMS. This rule contains the following defined terms:
- ball in play (35.4);
- caddie (35.7);
- Committee (35.11);
- course (35.13);
- fellow-competitor (35.12(B));
- hole (35.22);
- outside agency (35.36);
- rule (35.42); and
- teeing ground (35.50).

1.1 DESCRIPTION. Golf consists of playing a ball from the teeing ground into the hole according to the rules.

1.2 PRIMARY RULES

(A) Nothing to Affect a Ball in Play. Neither you nor your caddie may do anything that intentionally affects the position or movement of any ball in play, except as the rules say otherwise.

(B) Nothing to Affect Physical Conditions. You must play the course as you find it, without intentionally modifying it, unless the rules say otherwise. An action relating solely to course care does not violate this rule.

(c) If Another Rule Applies. An action expressly permitted or prohibited by another rule is subject to that specific rule, not this Rule 1.2.

(D) Penalty and Procedures. If you violate this Rule 1.2, you lose the hole in match play or receive a two-stroke penalty in stroke play. In stroke play, if you affect your ball's movement, you must play the ball from where it has stopped or come to rest after the movement. If your ball's movement was intentionally altered by a fellow-competitor or another outside agency, Rule 1.4 applies to you and the procedures in Rule 19.1(c) apply.

(E) **Serious Violation and Disqualification.** If you or your caddie's conduct violating this rule allows you or another player to gain a significant advantage or places another player (other than your partner) at a significant disadvantage, the Committee may disqualify you.

1.3 NO AGREEMENT TO IGNORE RULES. You cannot agree with anyone to ignore a rule or penalty. If you do this, you're disqualified. In stroke play, any action prohibited by Rule 10.2(c) (playing out of turn) or Rule 22.1(c) (not lifting a ball that might help a competitor) may also subject you to disqualification.

1.4 ISSUES NOT COVERED BY RULES. If any issue is not specifically covered by the rules, the Committee will make a decision based on fairness. See also Rule 34.3.

RULE 2. Match Play

2.0 DEFINED TERMS. This rule contains the following defined terms:
- caddie (35.7);
- Committee (35.11);
- handicap (35.20);
- hole (35.22);
- hole out (35.23);

- opponent (35.34);
- partner (35.37);
- penalty stroke (35.38);
- putting green (35.40);
- rule (35.42);
- side (35.44);
- stipulated round (35.46);
- stroke (35.47); and
- teeing ground (35.50).

2.1 SCORING AND WINNING THE MATCH

(A) Scoring by Holes. In match play, one side plays against another. The game is scored by holes. You win a hole by completing it in fewer strokes than your opponent. In a handicap match, the lower net score wins the hole. A hole is "halved" if you tie your opponent.

(B) Determining the Winner. You win a match if you lead by more holes than the number of holes remaining to be played. To determine the winner of a tie, the Committee may extend the stipulated round.

(c) Match-Play Terminology. Scoring in match play uses these terms: one side may be so many "holes up" (leading), or the sides may be "all square" (tied) with so many holes "to play" (remaining). You are "dormie" when you are leading by as many holes there are remaining.

2.2 PENALTIES

(A) Generally. The general penalty for violating a rule in match play is loss of hole — except as the rules say otherwise (see the Penalty Summary Chart in Appendix 1).

(B) After Holing Out. If you receive a penalty after

you've holed out and your opponent has been left with a stroke for the half, the hole is halved.

2.3 CONCESSION. When your opponent's ball is at rest, you may concede the next stroke, and your opponent will be considered to have holed out. You may concede a hole or a match at any time before it's over. Once a stroke, hole, or match is conceded, the concession can't be declined or withdrawn.

2.4 CLAIMS

(A) Making a Claim. If you believe that your opponent has violated the rules, you may make a claim by indicating that you want to apply the Rules of Golf. As long as there is no agreement to ignore the rules (see Rule 1.3), you may disregard an opponent's rules violation.

(B) Procedures and Decisions

(1) Specificity and Timeliness. For a claim to be considered by the Committee, you must notify your opponent that you are making a claim or requesting a ruling, and state the specific facts of the situation. You must make the claim before any player in the match plays from the next teeing ground — or, in the case of the last hole of the match, before all players in the match leave the putting green. If you first discover a fact giving rise to a claim after all the players in the match have left the final putting green, you may make a claim anytime before the match's result is officially announced.

(2) Promptness of Decision. If you make a claim against your opponent, the Committee should make a decision as soon as possible so that the status of the match will be certain.

(3) Continuing Play When Committee Unavailable. If a doubt or dispute arises between the players when no authorized Committee representative is available within a reasonable time, the players must continue the match without delay and await a decision. In match play, when you are doubtful of your rights or procedures, you cannot complete the hole with two balls.

(4) Late Claims. A late claim is governed by Rule 34.1(A)(2) (dealing with claims in match play).

2.5 INFORMATION ABOUT STROKES TAKEN

(A) Asking and Telling About Strokes Taken

(1) Asking. During or after the play of a hole, you may ask a player — or the player's caddie or partner — the number of strokes that player has taken for the hole, and that player must respond timely (see Rule 2.5(B)(1)).

(2) Disclosing a Penalty. If you've received a penalty, you must tell your opponent as soon as practicable, unless you're obviously proceeding under a rule involving a penalty and your opponent has seen this.

(3) Not Disclosing a Penalty. If you don't tell your opponent about a penalty, you're considered to have given wrong information, even if you're not aware that you've received the penalty. You're responsible for knowing the rules.

(B) Penalty for Giving Wrong Information

(1) While Playing a Hole. If you give or are considered to have given wrong information about the number of strokes taken during the play of a hole, there is no penalty if you correct the mistake before your opponent makes the next stroke. If you don't correct the wrong information, you lose the hole if your opponent makes a valid claim.

(2) After Completing a Hole. If you give or are considered to have given wrong information about the number of strokes you've taken on the hole just completed *and* this affects your opponent's understanding of the result of the hole, there is no penalty if you correct your mistake before any player in the match plays from the next teeing ground — or, in the case of the last hole of the match, before all players leave the putting green. If you don't correct the wrong information, you lose the previous hole if your opponent makes a valid claim.

RULE 3. Stroke Play

3.0 DEFINED TERMS. This rule contains the following defined terms:
- Committee (35.11);
- competitor (35.12);
- handicap (35.20);
- hole (35.22);
- hole out (35.23);
- penalty stroke (35.38);
- provisional ball (35.39);
- putting green (35.40);
- rule (35.42);
- scorer (35.43);
- stipulated round (35.46);
- stroke (35.47); and
- teeing ground (35.50).

3.1 SCORING

(A) Determining Winner. The competitor who plays the stipulated number of rounds in the fewest strokes wins. In a handicap competition, the competitor with the lowest net score for the stipulated rounds wins.

(B) Penalties. If you receive a penalty, you should inform your scorer and include all penalty strokes in your total.

3.2 PENALTIES

(A) General. The general penalty for breaching a rule in stroke play is two strokes, except as the rules say otherwise (see the Penalty Summary Chart in Appendix 1).

(B) Refusal to Comply. If you refuse to comply with a rule and your doing so affects another competitor's rights, you're disqualified.

3.3 FAILING TO HOLE OUT. If you don't hole out on a hole and fail to correct your mistake before making a stroke from the next teeing ground — or, in the case of the last hole of the round, before you leave the putting green — you're disqualified.

3.4 PLAYER'S DOUBT ABOUT PROCEDURES

(A) Player's Second-Ball Procedures

(1) Stroke Play. In stroke play only, if you're doubtful about your rights or about the correct procedure during the play of a hole, you may, without penalty, play and complete the hole with a second ball.

(2) Announcing Your Decision. Before taking any further action, such as making a stroke at your original ball, you should declare your decision to use this rule and the ball you prefer to score with, rules permitting. You may play either ball first.

(3) Action Before Decision. If you take further action before deciding to play two balls, your score with your original ball counts, but you aren't penalized for playing a second ball.

(4) Reporting to Committee. You must report the facts of your situation to the Committee before returning your score card. If you don't do this, you're disqualified.

(B) **Committee's Procedures to Determine Your Score When a Second Ball Has Been Played.** When you have used this Rule, the Committee will determine your score as follows:

(1) If You Followed These Procedures Correctly. If the ball that you selected in advance is played according to the rules, the score with that ball is your score for the hole, even if that score is higher. If the Rules don't permit the procedure used for your selected ball, then the score with the other ball counts, as long as you played it according to the rules.

(2) If You Did Not Follow These Procedures Correctly. If you take further action before announcing your decision to play two balls and which ball you wish to count, the score with your original ball will count, as long as you played it according to the rules.

(3) If Neither Ball Has Been Played According to the Rules. If the Rules don't permit the procedures used for both balls, your score with the original ball will count unless you have committed a serious rules violation by playing that ball from a wrong place. If you commit a serious rules violation playing one ball, the score with the other ball counts even though the Rules don't permit the procedure used for that ball. If you are guilty of a serious violation with both balls, you're disqualified.

(c) Notes.

(1) The phrasing "Rules permit the procedure used for a ball" means that after this Rule 3.4 is invoked, either (a) the original ball is played from where it had come to rest and play is permitted from that location, or (b) the Rules permit the procedure used for the ball and the ball is put into play in the proper manner and correct place as the rules provide.

(2) If the score with the original ball is supposed to count, but the original ball is not one of the balls being played, the first ball put into play is considered to be your "original" ball.

(3) After this Rule is invoked, strokes and penalty strokes incurred solely with the ball ruled not to count are disregarded.

(4) A second ball played under this Rule is not a provisional ball under Rule 27.2.

RULE 4. Clubs

4.0 DEFINED TERMS. This rule contains the following defined terms:
- club unfit for play (35.10);
- Committee (35.11);
- course (35.13);
- fellow-competitor (35.12(B));

- hole (35.22);
- partner (35.37);
- rule (35.42);
- stipulated round (35.46).
- stroke (35.47); and

4.1 ORIGINAL DESIGN AND CHANGES

(A) General. Your clubs must conform to the rules and the specifications in Appendix 2 of the official Rules of Golf published by the USGA. In a given competition, the Committee may require that your clubs be on the USGA list of conforming driver heads and iron grooves.

(B) No Change in Playing Characteristics. During a stipulated round, you must not purposely change the playing characteristics of a club.

(C) No Foreign Material. You must not put anything on the clubface to affect the ball's movement.

(D) Wear and Alteration. A club that conforms when new remains conforming after it wears through normal use. But any part of a club that has been purposely altered is considered new and must conform with the rules in its altered state.

(E) Penalty

(1) Stroke Made. If you make a stroke with a club that violates this Rule 4.1, you're disqualified.

(2) Stroke Not Made. During the stipulated round, if you carry a club that violates this Rule 4.1 but do not make a stroke with it, the following penalties apply:

(a) Match Play: After the hole where the violation is discovered, the score of the match is changed by deducting one hole for every hole where you violated this rule — up to a maximum of two holes per round.

(b) Stroke Play: You receive a two-stroke penalty for the first two holes where you violated this rule — up to a maximum of four strokes per round.

(c) Par and Bogey Competitions: See Rule 32.1(A)(2).

(d) Stableford Competition: See Rule 32.1(B)(2).

(e) Violation Discovered Between Holes: The penalty applies to the next hole.

(3) Declaring Club Out of Play. Any club carried in violation of this Rule must immediately be declared out of play to your opponent or fellow-competitor. If you don't do this, you're disqualified.

4.2 DAMAGED CLUBS: ALLOWABLE REPAIR AND REPLACEMENT

(A) Damage Before Round

(1) General Rule. You may use a club that has been damaged before a round only if the damaged club still conforms to the rules. Damage that occurred before the round may be repaired during the round if the playing characteristics aren't changed and play isn't delayed excessively.

(2) Penalty. If you violate this Rule 4.2(A), the penalties in Rule 4.1 apply.

(B) Damage in Normal Course of Play

(1) General Rule. If your club is damaged in the normal course of play during a stipulated round, you may:

(a) use the club for the rest of the stipulated round;

(b) repair the club as long as doing so does not delay play excessively; or

(c) replace the damaged club with any club, but only if four conditions are met: the club must be unfit for play; the replacement club must not have been selected for play by someone else playing the course; replacement must not delay play excessively; and the replacement club cannot be made by assembling components carried by or for you during the stipulated round.

(2) Penalty. If you violate this Rule 4.2(B), the penalties in Rule 4.3(C) apply.

(C) **Damage Other Than in Normal Course of Play**

(1) General Rule. During a stipulated round, if damage occurs other than in the normal course of play (as when a club is damaged in anger) and changes a club's playing characteristics or makes it nonconforming, the club must not be used or replaced during the round.

(2) Penalty. If you violate this Rule 4.2(C), you're disqualified.

4.3 FOURTEEN-CLUB MAXIMUM

(A) **Selecting and Adding Clubs.** You're limited to fourteen clubs when starting a stipulated round — and to the clubs you've selected for that round. If you started with fewer than fourteen clubs, you may add clubs during the stipulated round, but you must not exceed fourteen. When adding clubs, you must not delay play excessively, borrow any club selected for play by anyone else playing the course, or assemble club components carried by or for you during the stipulated round.

(B) **Restrictions on Sharing Clubs.** You may share clubs with your partner, but only if all the clubs that you and your partners carry, when added together, don't exceed fourteen.

(C) **Penalty.** If you violate Rule 4.3(A) or (B), the following penalties apply:

(1) Match Play: After the hole where the violation is discovered, the score of the match is changed by deducting one hole for every hole where you violated this rule — up to a maximum of two holes per round.

(2) Stroke Play: You receive a two-stroke penalty for the first two holes where you violated this rule — up to a maximum of four strokes per round.

(3) Par and Bogey Competitions: See Rule 32.1(A)(2).

(4) Stableford Competition: See Rule 32.1(B)(2).

(5) Violation Discovered Between Holes: The penalty applies to the previous hole

(D) **Extra Clubs Declared out of Play.** Any club carried or used in violation of Rules 4.3(A) or (B) must immediately be declared out of play and cannot then be used during the round. If you violate this Rule 4.3(D), you're disqualified.

RULE 5. The Ball

5.0 DEFINED TERMS. This rule contains the following defined terms:

- ball unfit for play (35.5);
- Committee (35.11);
- fellow-competitor (35.12(B)(C));
- hole (35.22);
- opponent (35.34);
- penalty stroke (35.38);
- scorer (35.43); and
- stroke (35.47).

5.1 GENERAL. Your ball must conform to the specifications in Appendix 3 of the official Rules of Golf published by the USGA.

5.2 FOREIGN-MATERIAL RESTRICTION

(A) No Foreign Material. You must not put anything on the ball to intentionally affect its playing characteristics.

(B) Penalty. If you violate Rule 5.1 or 5.2, you're disqualified.

5.3 DAMAGED BALL

(A) Procedures

(1) Unfit Ball. If you believe your ball has become unfit for play while you're playing a hole, you may lift it without penalty to determine whether it is unfit.

(2) Announcing Your Intent. Before lifting the ball, you must announce to your opponent, scorer, or fellow-competitor what you're doing and mark the ball's position. You may then lift the ball and look at it, but you must not clean it. You must also give your opponent, scorer, or fellow-competitor an opportunity to look at the ball and watch your lifting and re-placement.

(3) Failure to Follow Procedures. If you don't follow this procedure, or if you lift your ball without reason to believe it is unfit for play, you receive a one-stroke penalty.

(4) Substitution of Ball. If the ball has become unfit for play during that hole, you may substitute another ball in the original ball's position. Otherwise, the original ball must be re-placed. If the original lie has been altered, see Rule 20.3(C).

(5) Disputed Claim. An opponent, scorer, or fellow-competitor who disputes a claim of unfitness must do so before you play another ball.

(B) Penalty. If you violate this Rule 5.3 by improperly substituting a ball, you lose the hole in match play or receive a two-stroke penalty in stroke play. If you receive the general penalty in this Rule 5.3, no additional penalty for procedural violations is applied.

5.4 BROKEN BALL. If your ball breaks into pieces after a stroke, the stroke is canceled and you must play a ball without penalty from the spot where you played the original ball (see Rule 20.5).

RULE 6.
The Player's Responsibilities

6.0 DEFINED TERMS. This rule contains the following defined terms:
- advice (35.3);
- caddie (35.7);
- Committee (35.11);
- course (35.13);
- equipment (35.14);
- handicap (35.20);
- hole (35.22);
- loose impediment (35.28);
- movable obstruction (35.33(B));
- move (35.30);
- opponent (35.34);
- penalty stroke (35.38);
- rule (35.42);

- scorer (35.43);
- stipulated round (35.46);
- substituted ball (35.48); and
- stroke (35.47).

6.1 RULES. You and your caddie are responsible for knowing the rules and conditions of competition.

6.2 HANDICAP. The following rules apply in a handicap competition.

(A) Match Play. You're responsible for knowing your handicap, your opponent's handicap, and the holes where handicap strokes are to be given or received. If you begin a match declaring a higher handicap than you actually have, and this declaration affects the number of strokes given or received, you're disqualified. If the number of strokes given or received is not affected, you must play off your declared handicap, even if you declared a handicap that's too low.

(B) Stroke Play. You're responsible for your handicap being recorded on your scorecard before returning it to the Committee. If no handicap has been recorded, or if your handicap is higher than what you're entitled to and this affects the number of strokes you received, you're disqualified from the handicap competition. Otherwise, the score stands.

6.3 STARTING TIME AND GROUPS

(A) Starting Time. You must start at the time set by the Committee.

(B) Penalty. If you arrive at your starting point ready to play within five minutes after your starting time, the penalty for failing to start on time is loss of the first hole to be played in match play or two strokes

at the first hole to be played in stroke play. Otherwise, you're disqualified.
- **(c) Exception.** If the Committee determines that extraordinary circumstances excuse your tardiness, you are not penalized.
- **(d) Par, Bogey, and Stableford Competitions.** See Rule 32.
- **(e) Groups.** In stroke play, you must remain with the group set by the Committee unless the Committee authorizes a change. If you don't, you're disqualified.

6.4 CADDIE

- **(a) Permitted Actions.** You may be assisted by a caddie, who may carry your equipment, give advice, and otherwise help you according to the rules. Your caddie may also search for your ball, repair ball marks, remove loose impediments as allowed by Rules 23.1 and 16.1(A)(1), mark the position of your ball, clean your ball, and remove movable obstructions, even without your authority.
- **(b) Caddie Violations.** If your caddie violates a rule during a stipulated round, you receive the applicable penalty.
- **(c) Committee Restriction.** The Committee may prohibit use of a caddie or restrict your choice of caddie in the conditions of a competition (see Rule 33.1(A)).
- **(d) Only One Caddie.** You may have only one caddie at any time, but you may change caddies at any time during the stipulated round.
- **(e) Penalty.** If you violate Rule 6.4(D), the following penalties apply:

    (1) Match Play: After the hole where the violation

is discovered, the score of the match is changed by deducting one hole for every hole where you violated this rule — up to a maximum of two holes per round.

(2) Stroke Play: You receive a two-stroke penalty for the first two holes where you violated this rule — up to a maximum of four strokes per round.

(3) Par and Bogey Competitions: See Rule 32.1(A)(2).

(4) Stableford Competition: See Rule 32.1(B)(2).

(5) Violation Discovered Between Holes: The penalty also applies to the next hole.

(6) Second Violation: If you violate this Rule 6.4(D) twice during a stipulated round, you're disqualified.

6.5 BALL. You're responsible for playing the right ball. You should put an identifying mark on your ball.

6.6 SCORING IN STROKE PLAY

(A) Recording Scores. After each hole, the scorer should record your score. After the round, the scorer must sign the card and give it to you. If more than one scorer records your scores, each one must sign for the holes that he or she recorded.

(B) Signing and Returning Card. You are responsible for ensuring that the scorer has signed the card, for checking your score for each hole, and for settling any doubtful points with the Committee. You must then sign the card and return it to the Committee.

(C) Penalty. If you violate Rule 6.6(B), you're disqualified.

(D) No Altering Card. Once a card has been returned to the Committee, it can't be altered.

(E) Wrong Score for Hole. You're responsible for the

correct score for each hole. If you return a score for any hole lower than the number of strokes actually taken, you're disqualified. If you return a score for any hole showing a higher score than the number of strokes actually taken, the score stands.

(F) Exception. If you return a score for any hole lower than your actual score because you failed to include one or more penalty strokes that, before returning your scorecard, you didn't know you had incurred, you are not disqualified. In these circumstances, you receive the penalty prescribed by the applicable Rule and an additional two-stroke penalty for each hole where you violated Rule 6.6(E). This exception doesn't apply when the actual penalty is disqualification.

(G) Committee Responsibilities. The Committee is responsible for adding the total score and applying your handicap.

6.7 UNDUE DELAY AND SLOW PLAY

(A) Prompt Play. During a round, you must play promptly and according to any pace-of-play guidelines set by the Committee. The Committee's guidelines may include maximum time periods for completing a stroke, a hole, or a stipulated round.

(B) Penalty. If you violate this Rule 6.7, the penalties are as follows (unless modified by the Committee):

(1) for the first violation, you lose the hole in match play or receive a two-stroke penalty in stroke play;

(2) for the second violation, you're disqualified;

(3) for bogey and par competitions, see Rule 32.1(A)(2).

(4) for Stableford competitions, see Rule 32.1(B)(2).

(C) Deferred Penalty. If you unduly delay play between holes, the penalty applies to the next hole.

(D) Alternative Penalty.

(1) Match Play. In a given match-play competition, the Committee may modify this penalty as follows:

(a) for the first violation, loss of hole;

(b) for the second violation, loss of hole; and,

(c) for any further violation, disqualification.

(2) Stroke Play. In a given stroke-play competition, the Committee may modify this penalty as follows:

(a) for the first violation, one stroke;

(b) for the second violation, two strokes; and

(c) for any further violation, disqualification.

6.8 STOPPING PLAY AND RESUMING PLAY

(A) Player Stopping Play

(1) When Permitted. You must play continuously unless:

(a) the Committee has suspended play;

(b) you believe there is dangerous lightning nearby (though bad weather by itself is not a valid reason to stop play);

(c) you are seeking a rules decision from the Committee (see Rules 2.4 and 34.3); or

(d) you suddenly become ill or have some other good reason.

(2) Procedure and Penalty. If you stop play without Committee permission, you must report to the Committee as soon as practicable. If the Committee considers your reason satisfactory, you receive no penalty. Otherwise, you're disqualified.

(3) Match-Play Exception. Players who agree to stop match play will not be disqualified unless their actions delay the competition.

(4) Leaving Course. Leaving the course does not necessarily constitute stopping play.

(B) Committee Suspends Play

(1) Between Holes. If the Committee suspends play while the players in a match or group are between holes, the players must not resume play until the Committee orders play resumed.

(2) During Hole. If the Committee suspends play while the players are playing a hole, they may stop when play is suspended or continue play of that hole only, as long as they do so without delay.

(3) Exception for Dangerous Situations. As a condition of a competition, the Committee may provide that in potentially dangerous situations (as when lightning is nearby) play must be stopped immediately. If you violate this rule in circumstances that do not warrant waiving a disqualification penalty, you're disqualified (see Rule 33.1(B)).

(4) Penalty. If you violate this Rule 6.8(B) or don't stop or resume play as ordered by the Committee, you're disqualified.

(c) Lifting Ball When Play Is Suspended

(1) Procedures. When you stop playing a hole, you may lift your ball without penalty only if the Committee has suspended play or there is a good reason to lift it. Before lifting the ball, you must mark its position. If you stop play and lift your ball without specific permission from the Committee, when reporting to the Committee you must report the lifting of the ball.

(2) Penalty. You are penalized one stroke if you:

(a) lift your ball without good reason;

(b) don't mark the position of the ball before lifting it; or

(c) don't report the lifting of the ball.

(D) Procedures When Play Is Resumed. You must resume play when the Committee says to resume, from the place where you stopped. Proceed as follows:

(1) Having Chosen to Lift. If you were entitled to lift your ball under Rule 6.8(C) and you did so, place the original ball or a substituted ball on the spot from which the original ball was lifted.

(2) Having Chosen Not to Lift. If you were entitled to lift your ball under Rule 6.8(C) but you didn't, you may then mark, lift, clean, and re-place the ball, or substitute a ball on the spot from which the original ball was lifted.

(3) Not Having Been Entitled to Lift. If you were not entitled to lift your ball under Rule 6.8(C), the original ball must be re-placed.

(4) Ball Moved While Play Suspended. If your ball or ball marker was moved while play was stopped (including by wind or water), a ball or ball marker must be placed on the spot from which the original ball or ball marker was moved.

(5) Not Certain About Spot. If you can't be certain about the precise spot to place your ball under this rule, you must place your ball on the estimated spot. Rule 20.3(B)(2) doesn't apply.

(6) Penalty. If you violate this Rule 6.8(D), you lose the hole in match play or receive a two-stroke penalty in stroke play. If you receive the general penalty for violating Rule 6.8(D), no additional penalty under Rule 6.8(C) is applied.

RULE 7. Practice

7.0 DEFINED TERMS. This rule contains the following defined terms:
- Committee (35.11);
- course (35.13);
- hazard (35.21);
- hole (35.22);
- putting green (35.40);
- stipulated round (35.46);
- stroke (35.47); and
- teeing ground (35.50).

7.1 BEFORE AND BETWEEN ROUNDS

(A) **Match Play.** On any day of a match-play competition, you may practice on the competition course before a round.

(B) **Stroke Play**

   (1) Restriction. You must not practice on the competition course or test the surface of a putting green on the competition course by rolling a ball or by roughening or scraping its surface:

   (a) before a round or playoff on the day of a competition; or

   (b) between rounds when rounds of a competition are played over consecutive days.

   (2) First-Tee Exception. Before starting a round or a playoff, you may practice putting or chipping on or near the first teeing ground or any practice area.

   (3) Penalty. If you violate this Rule 7.1(B), you're disqualified.

(C) **Exception Note.** In the conditions of competition, the Committee may prohibit practice on the competition course on any day of a match-play competition or allow practice on any day or between rounds of a stroke-play competition.

7.2 RESTRICTIONS DURING ROUND

(A) General Rule. You must not make a practice stroke during the stipulated round.

(B) Exception Between Holes. Between the play of two holes, you may practice putting or chipping on or near the putting green of the previous hole, a practice putting green, or the teeing ground of the next hole, as long as the practice stroke is not made from a hazard and doesn't unduly delay play.

(C) Notes

(1) Committee Restriction. As a condition of a competition, the Committee may prohibit practice on or near, or rolling a ball on, the putting green of the previous hole.

(2) After Completion. A stroke made in continuing a hole that has already been decided is not a practice stroke.

(3) Practice Swing. A practice swing is not a practice stroke. You may take a practice swing at any place, as long as you don't otherwise violate the rules.

(D) Penalty. If you violate this Rule 7.2, you lose the hole in match play or receive a two-stroke penalty in stroke play. If your violation occurs between holes, the penalty applies to the next hole.

7.3 DURING SUSPENDED PLAY.

(A) General Rule. During a Committee suspension, and before resuming play, you may practice anywhere other than on the competition course. You may also practice either as this Rule 7 provides or as the Committee permits.

(B) Penalty. If you violate this Rule 7.3, you lose the hole in match play or receive a two-stroke penalty in stroke play.

RULE 8.
Advice and Indicating Line of Play

8.0 DEFINED TERMS. This rule contains the following defined terms:
- advice (35.3);
- caddie (35.7);
- Committee (35.11);
- flagstick (35.15);
- hole (35.22);
- line of play (35.26);
- line of putt (35.27);
- partner (35.37);
- putting green (35.40);
- stipulated round (35.46); and
- stroke (35.47).

8.1 ADVICE RESTRICTIONS. During a stipulated round, you must not advise anyone in the competition except your partner. You may ask for advice only from your partner, your caddie, or your partner's caddie.

8.2 INDICATING LINE OF PLAY

(A) Ball Anywhere But on Putting Green

(1) Before the Stroke. Before the stroke, you may have the line of play indicated to you by anyone.

Any mark placed either by you or with your knowledge for the purpose of indicating the line of play must be removed before the stroke is made.

(2) During the Stroke. During the stroke, no one can be positioned on or close to the line of play—or an extension of the line beyond the hole or behind the ball—for the purpose of indicating the line of play.

(3) Flagstick Exception. As specified in Rule 17.1, the flagstick may be attended or even held up during the stroke to indicate the position of the hole.

(B) **Ball on Putting Green**

(1) Before the Stroke. Before a stroke, you, your partner, or either of your caddies may point out a line for putting, but they must not touch the putting green. No mark may be placed anywhere for the purpose of indicating the line of putt. See also Rule 16.1(A) for touching the line of putt.

(2) During the Stroke. During the stroke, you can't allow your partner or either of your caddies to be positioned on or close to the line of putt or an extension of the line behind the ball.

(C) **Exception.** You aren't penalized under this Rule 8.2 if your caddie, partner, or partner's caddie is accidentally positioned on or close to an extension of the line of play or line of putt behind the ball.

8.3 ADVICE EXCEPTION FOR TEAM COMPETITIONS.

As a condition of a team competition, the Committee may permit each team to appoint one person who may give advice (including pointing out the line of putt) to members of that team. The Committee may lay down conditions relating to the appointment, identification, and permitted conduct of this person.

8.4 PENALTY. If you violate this Rule 8, you lose the hole in match play or receive a two-stroke penalty in stroke play.

RULE 9.
Information About Strokes Taken

[Deleted and incorporated more logically into Rules 3.1(B) and 2.5]

RULE 10. Order of Play

10.0 DEFINED TERMS. This rule contains the following defined terms:
- best-ball (35.17(E));
- Committee (35.11);
- competitor (35.12);
- four-ball match play (35.17(F));
- four-ball stroke play (see Rule 35.18(C));
- hole (35.22);
- honor (35.24);
- opponent (35.34);
- out of bounds (35.35);
- provisional ball (35.39);
- side (35.44);
- stroke (35.47);
- tee (35.49);
- teeing ground (35.50); and
- water hazard (35.52).

10.1 MATCH PLAY

(A) Ball on the Teeing Ground

(1) First Hole. The side with the honor at the first teeing ground is determined by the draw order. Without a draw, the honor is decided by lot.

(2) Later Holes. The side that wins a hole has the honor at the next teeing ground. If a hole has been halved, the honor remains the same as on the previous hole.

(B) Ball Anywhere but the Teeing Ground

(1) Proper Order. When balls are in play, the ball farthest from the hole must be played first. If two or more balls are the same distance from the hole, the ball to be played first is decided by lot.

(2) Original Ball Not Played As It Lies. When it becomes known that you aren't going to play your original ball as it lies and you are required to play a ball as nearly as possible from where the original ball was last played (as with a ball lost or out of bounds), the order of play is determined by the spot from which the previous stroke was made. When you are allowed to play from a spot other than where the previous stroke was made (as with some water-hazard options), the order of play depends on where the original ball came to rest.

(3) Exception. Rule 30.3(B) (best-ball and four-ball match play) is an exception to Rule 10.1(B)(1) and (2).

(C) Playing Out of Turn. If you play when your opponent should have played, the opponent may immediately require you to cancel the stroke and to play a ball in correct order, without penalty, as nearly as possible from the spot where the canceled stroke was made (see Rule 20.5).

10.2 STROKE PLAY

(A) Ball on the Teeing Ground

(1) First Hole. The competitor who has the honor at the first teeing ground is determined by the draw order. Without a draw, the honor is decided by lot.

(2) Later Holes. The competitor with the lowest score on a hole has the honor at the next tee. The competitor with the second lowest score plays next, and so on. If two or more competitors have the same score on a hole, they play from the next teeing ground in the same order as on the previous teeing ground. For the order of play in handicap bogey, par, and Stableford competitions, see Rule 32.1.

(B) Ball Anywhere but the Teeing Ground

(1) Proper Order. When balls are in play, the ball farthest from the hole is played first. If two or more balls are the same distance from the hole, the ball played first is decided by lot.

(2) Original Ball Not Played As It Lies. When it becomes known that you aren't going to play your original ball as it lies and you are required to play a ball as nearly as possible from where the original ball was last played (as with a ball lost or out of bounds), the order of play is determined by the spot from where the previous stroke was made. When you are allowed to play from a spot other than where the previous stroke was made (as with some water-hazard options), the order of play depends on where the original ball came to rest.

(3) Exceptions. Rule 22 (ball interfering with or assisting play) and 31.4 (four-ball stroke play).

(C) Playing Out of Turn. If someone plays out of turn, there is no penalty and the ball is played as it lies.

But if the Committee determines that competitors have agreed to play out of turn to give one of them an advantage, they are disqualified. (For incorrect order of play in foursome stroke play, see Rule 29.3.) For a stroke made while another ball is in motion after a stroke from a putting green, see Rule 16.1(F).

10.3 PROVISIONAL BALL OR SECOND BALL FROM TEEING GROUND. If you play a provisional ball or a second ball from a teeing ground, you should do so after your opponent or fellow-competitors have played. If more than one player plays a provisional ball from the teeing ground, the original order of play remains the same. If you play a provisional ball or second ball out of turn, Rule 10.1(C) or 10.2(C) applies.

RULE 11. Teeing Ground

11.0 DEFINED TERMS. This rule contains the following defined terms:
- ball in play (35.4);
- hole (35.22);
- line of play (35.26);
- opponent (35.34);
- putting green (35.40);
- stance (35.45);
- stroke (35.47);
- tee (35.49); and
- teeing ground (35.50).

11.1 TEEING THE BALL. When you put a ball in play from the teeing ground, your ball must be placed on a conforming tee, on the ground, on an irregularity of ground created by you, or on sand or some other natural substance. You may remove dew, frost, or water from the teeing ground. You may stand outside the teeing ground to play a ball within it. If you make a stroke at a ball teed on a nonconforming object or teed in a manner not allowed by this Rule 11.1, you're disqualified.

11.2 TEE-MARKERS. Before you make your first stroke with any ball from the teeing ground, the tee-markers are considered to be fixed. If you move a tee-marker or allow it to be moved to avoid interference with your stance, the area of your intended swing, or your line of play, you receive the penalty for violating Rule 13.2.

11.3 BALL FALLING OFF TEE. If a ball is not in play and you knock it off a tee when addressing it, you may re-tee it without penalty. If you make a stroke in these circumstances, whether or not the ball is moving, the stroke counts but there is no penalty.

11.4 PLAYING FROM OUTSIDE TEEING GROUND

(A) Match Play. When starting a hole, if you play a ball from outside the teeing ground, your opponent may immediately require you to cancel the stroke and then play a ball from within the teeing ground without a penalty.

(B) Stroke Play

(1) General. When starting a hole, if you play a ball from outside the teeing ground, you are penalized two strokes and must then play a ball from within the teeing ground. The stroke made from outside the teeing ground and any later strokes you make before correcting your mistake do not count in your score.

(2) Required Correction. If you make a stroke from the next teeing ground without first correcting your mistake — or leave the putting green of the last hole of your round without first declaring your intention to correct your mistake — you're disqualified.

11.5 PLAYING FROM WRONG TEEING GROUND. Rule 11.4 applies.

RULE 12.
Searching for and Identifying Ball

12.0 DEFINED TERMS. This rule contains the following defined terms:
- abnormal ground condition (35.1);
- casual water (35.8);
- course (35.13);
- fellow-competitor (35.12(B), (C));
- ground under repair (35.19);
- hazard (35.21);
- line of play (35.26);
- loose impediment (35.28);
- move (35.30);
- obstruction (35.33);
- opponent (35.34);
- scorer (35.43);
- stroke (35.47); and
- water hazard (35.52).

12.1 SEARCHING FOR BALL AND SEEING BALL

(A) General Rule. When searching for your ball anywhere on the course, you may touch or bend long grass, bushes, or similar growth, but only to the extent necessary to find or identify the ball. You must not improve the lie of the ball, the area of your intended swing, or your line of play by these actions. Generally, if the ball moves during a search, you receive a penalty under Rule 18.2(A) unless subsection (B), (C), (D), or (E) of this Rule 12.1 specifically applies. There is no right to see your ball when making a stroke.

(B) **Sand Covering a Ball.** If a ball might be covered by sand anywhere on the course, you may touch or move enough sand to find or identify the ball. If the ball is yours, you must re-create the original lie by replacing the sand, but you may leave a small part of the ball visible. If you move the ball while searching for or identifying your ball in sand, or re-creating the lie, you receive no penalty, but the ball must be re-placed and the original lie re-created.

(C) **Loose Impediments Covering a Ball in Hazard.** If a ball might be covered by loose impediments in a hazard, you may touch or remove only enough loose impediments to find or identify the ball. If the ball is yours, you must replace the loose impediments, but you may leave a small part of the ball visible. If you move the ball while removing loose impediments under this rule, you are penalized under Rule 18.2(A). If you move the ball while replacing loose impediments after identifying the ball as yours, you receive no penalty, but you must re-place the ball. For removal of loose impediments outside a hazard, see Rule 23.

(D) **Ball in Water in a Water Hazard.** If a ball might be in water in a water hazard, you may probe for it with a club or otherwise. If you move the ball in water during this act, the ball must be re-placed unless you decide to proceed under Rule 26.1. There is no penalty for moving the ball as long as the movement of the ball is directly caused by the specific act of probing for it in the water. Otherwise, you receive a penalty stroke under Rule 18.2(A).

(E) Ball in Obstruction or Abnormal Ground Condition. If you accidentally move a ball in an obstruction or an abnormal ground condition (such as casual water or ground under repair) during a search, there is no penalty. The ball must be replaced unless you decide to proceed under Rule 24.1(A)(3), Rule 24.2(B), or Rule 25.1(B). After replacing the ball, you may still use these rules if applicable.

(F) Penalty. If you violate this Rule 12.1, you lose the hole in match play or receive a two-stroke penalty in stroke play.

12.2 IDENTIFYING BALL

(A) General Rule. If you believe that a ball at rest is yours and you cannot identify it, you may lift the ball to identify it. You may clean it only to the extent needed to identify it. If the ball is yours, it must be re-placed.

(B) Procedures. Before lifting the ball, you must announce to your opponent, scorer, or fellow-competitor what you're doing and mark the ball's position. You may then lift the ball to identify it. Your opponent, scorer, or fellow-competitor must be given an opportunity to observe the lifting and re-placement. If the original lie has been altered, see Rule 20.3(C).

(c) Procedural Penalties. You are penalized one stroke if you lift your ball to identify it without having a good reason to do so; lift your ball without announcing your intentions; fail to mark its position; fail to give your opponent, your scorer, or a fellow-competitor an opportunity to observe your actions; or clean your ball more than needed to identify it. If you are required to re-place a ball and don't, you receive the general penalty for violating Rule 12, but no further penalty under this Rule 12.2.

RULE 13. Playing the Ball As It Lies

13.0 DEFINED TERMS. This rule contains the following defined terms:
- addressing the ball (35.2);
- caddie (35.7);
- course (35.13);
- hazard (35.21);
- hole (35.22);
- integral part of the course (35.33(A)(3));
- line of play (35.26);
- loose impediment (35.28);
- obstruction (35.33);
- out of bounds (35.35);
- rule (35.42);
- stance (35.45);
- stroke (35.47); and
- through the green (35.51).

13.1 GENERAL. You must play the ball as it lies, without modifying the course, except as the rules say otherwise.

13.2 IMPROVING LIE, STANCE, OR SWING, OR LINE OF PLAY THROUGH THE GREEN

(A) General Restriction

(1) Improvements. You must not improve the position or lie of your ball, the area of your intended stance or swing, your line of play (including a reasonable extension of that line beyond the hole), or the area in which you are to drop or place a ball by taking any of the following actions:

(a) moving, bending, or breaking anything growing or fixed (including immovable obstructions and objects defining out of bounds);

(b) creating or eliminating irregularities of surface;

(c) removing or pressing down sand, loose soil, replaced divots, or other cut turf placed in position; or

(d) removing dew, frost, or water.

(2) Address. When addressing your ball, you may ground your club lightly, but you must not press it on the ground.

(B) Exception

(1) Fairness. You may take the actions in Rule 13.2(A) as long as they occur only while fairly taking your stance, or in making a stroke or the backward movement of your club for a stroke and the stroke is made.

(2) Other Areas of Course. For restrictions on improving the position or lie of the ball on other specific areas of the course, see the following rules:

(a) Teeing the Ball (Rule 11.1);
(b) Ball in Hazard (Rule 13.4); and
(c) Ball on Putting Green (Rule 16.1).

13.3 BUILDING STANCE. You may place your feet firmly in taking your stance, but you must not build a stance.

13.4 BALL IN HAZARD

(A) General Restrictions. Before making a stroke from a hazard, you must not:

(1) test the condition of the hazard or any similar hazard;

(2) touch the ground or water in the hazard with your hand or a club; or

(3) touch a loose impediment in the hazard.

(B) Exceptions

(1) You may search for a ball in a hazard as described in Rule 12.1.

(2) You may:

(a) place your clubs in a hazard; or

(b) touch the ground, loose impediments in any hazard, or water in a hazard while removing an obstruction; while measuring, retrieving, marking the position of, lifting, placing, or re-placing a ball under any rule; or if you're falling or trying to avoid falling.

(3) The actions described in (1) and (2) don't result in penalty only if you don't do anything that constitutes testing the condition of the hazard or improving your lie.

(4) You or your caddie may smooth sand or soil in the hazard at any time as long as you do so for the sole purpose of caring for the course and nothing is done to improve the ball's lie or to help your stance or line of play for your next stroke. If a ball you've played from a hazard is outside the hazard after the stroke, you or your caddie may smooth sand or soil in the hazard without restriction.

(5) If you make a stroke from a hazard and your ball comes to rest in a different hazard, the restrictions of this Rule 13.4 don't apply to any actions you take in the first hazard after the stroke.

(6) You may touch any obstruction, any construction declared to be an integral part of the course, or any grass, bush, tree, or other growing thing at any time, including at address or in the backswing.

13.5 PENALTY. If you violate this Rule 13, you lose the hole in match play or receive a two-stroke penalty in stroke play.

RULE 14.
Striking the Ball; Artificial Devices

14.0 DEFINED TERMS. This rule contains the following defined terms:
- addressing the ball (35.2);
- caddie (35.7);
- Committee (35.11);
- equipment (35.14);
- hole (35.22);
- move (35.30);
- partner (35.37);
- penalty stroke (35.38);
- rule (35.42);

- stipulated round (35.46);
- stroke (35.47); and
- water hazard (35.52).

14.1 STRIKE WITH CLUBHEAD ONLY. You must strike the ball with the head of the club. You can't push it, scrape it, or spoon it. If you violate this Rule 14.1, you lose the hole in match play or receive a two-stroke penalty in stroke play.

14.2 ANCHORING THE CLUB IS NOT ALLOWED. While making a stroke, you must not anchor the club, either directly or by using an anchor point. A club is considered directly anchored if you intentionally hold the club or a gripping hand in contact with any part of your body, but you may hold the club or a gripping hand against your hand or forearm. An anchor point exists if you intentionally hold a forearm in contact with any part of your body to establish a gripping hand as a stable point around which the club may be swung with your other hand. If you violate this Rule 14.2, you lose the hole in match play or receive a two-stroke penalty in stroke play.

14.3 NO ASSISTANCE. When making a stroke, you must not accept anyone's physical help or protection from the elements. If you violate this Rule 14.3, you lose the hole in match play or receive a two-stroke penalty in stroke play. [Note: official Rule 14.2b has been incorporated into 8.2(A)(2) and 8.2(B)(2).]

14.4 ARTIFICIAL DEVICES, UNUSUAL EQUIPMENT, AND ABNORMAL USE OF EQUIPMENT.

(A) Restriction. Except as allowed in Rule 14.4(B), during a stipulated round you must not use any artificial device or unusual equipment. Nor may you use any equipment in an abnormal manner:

(1) that might help you make a stroke or help your play in any other way;

(2) to gauge or measure distance or conditions that could affect your play; or

(3) that might help you grip the club.

(B) Exceptions.

(1) You may wear plain gloves, use resin powder and similar items, or wrap a towel or handkerchief around the grip.

(2) You may use an artificial device if:

(a) it is designed to accommodate a medical condition;

(b) you have a good medical reason to use it; and

(c) the Committee determines that using it doesn't give you an unfair advantage.

(3) The Committee may make a local rule allowing you to use a distance-measuring device.

(C) Penalty. For a first violation of this Rule 14.4, you lose the hole in match play or receive a two-stroke penalty in stroke play. For any later violation, you're disqualified.

14.5 MULTIPLE STRIKES. If your club strikes the ball more than once during a stroke, you must count the stroke and add a penalty stroke, making two strokes in all. You must play the ball as it lies.

14.6 PLAYING A MOVING BALL

(A) Restriction. You must not play your ball while it is moving.

(B) Exceptions. You're allowed to play a moving ball only in the following specific circumstances:

(1) if your ball is falling off a tee (Rule 11.3);

(2) if you inadvertently strike the ball more than once (Rule 14.5); and

(3) if your ball is moving in water in a water hazard (Rule 14.7).

(c) If Ball Moves After Stroke Begins

(1) General Rule. If the ball begins to move after you have begun the stroke or the backward movement of your club for the stroke, you are not penalized for playing a moving ball, but you may be penalized under Rule 18.2 (ball at rest moved by player) if that Rule applies.

(2) Purposely Deflected. When a ball is purposely deflected or stopped by a player, partner, or caddie, Rule 1.2(A) applies.

(D) Penalty. If you violate this Rule 14.6, you lose the hole in match play or receive a two-stroke penalty in stroke play.

14.7 BALL MOVING IN WATER IN A WATER HAZARD

(A) Restrictions. When your ball is moving in water in a water hazard, you may, without penalty, make a stroke at the moving ball, but you must not delay making your stroke in order to allow the wind or current to improve the ball's position. A ball moving in water in a water hazard may be lifted if you decide to proceed under Rule 26.

(B) Penalty. If you violate this Rule 14.6, you lose the hole in match play or receive a two-stroke penalty in stroke play.

RULE 15.
Substituted Ball; Wrong Ball

15.0 DEFINED TERMS. This rule contains the following defined terms:
- ball in play (35.4);
- competitor (35.12);
- hazard (35.21);
- hole (35.22);
- hole out (35.23);
- opponent (35.34);
- putting green (35.40);
- rule (35.42);
- stroke (35.47);
- substituted ball (35.48);
- teeing ground (35.50); and
- wrong ball (35.53).

15.1 GENERAL RULE FOR SUBSTITUTED BALL

(A) General Rule. You must hole out with the ball played from the teeing ground unless the ball is lost or out of bounds, or you substitute another ball. You may substitute a ball when proceeding under a rule that allows you to play, drop, or place another ball to complete a hole. If you substitute another ball when not allowed (including when you unintentionally substitute by dropping or placing a wrong ball), that ball is not a wrong ball; it becomes the ball in play.

(B) Improper Substitution Penalty. If an improper substitution is not corrected as allowed in Rule 20.6, you lose the hole in match play — or receive a two-stroke penalty in stroke play — and must complete the hole with the substituted ball.

(c) Penalty Limitation. If you receive a penalty for playing from a wrong place, there is no additional penalty for improperly substituting a ball.

15.2 WRONG BALL IN MATCH PLAY

(a) General Penalty. If you make a stroke at a wrong ball, you lose the hole.

(b) Procedures. If the wrong ball belongs to another player, its owner must place a ball on the spot from which the wrong ball was first played. (For returning the ball, see Rule 20.3.)

(c) Exchanged Balls. If you and your opponent exchange balls during the play of a hole, the first to play the wrong ball loses the hole. When this cannot be determined, the hole is played out with the balls exchanged, and no penalty is received.

(d) Exception. You receive no penalty if you make a stroke at a wrong ball moving in water in a water hazard (Rule 14.6). The stroke doesn't count toward your score. But you must correct your mistake by playing the correct ball.

15.3 WRONG BALL IN STROKE PLAY

(a) General Penalty. If you make a stroke at a wrong ball, you are penalized two strokes.

(b) Procedures. Strokes you make at a wrong ball do not count in your score. If the wrong ball belongs to another competitor, its owner must place a ball on the spot from which the wrong ball was first played. (For returning the ball, see Rule 20.3.)

(c) Required Correction. You must correct the mistake by playing your ball. If you don't correct your mistake before you make a stroke from the next tee — or, in the case of the last hole of the round, if you don't declare your intention to correct your mistake before leaving the putting green — you're disqualified.

(D) Exception. You receive no penalty if you make a stroke at a wrong ball moving in water in a water hazard (Rule 14.6). The stroke doesn't count toward your score. But you must correct your mistake by playing the correct ball.

RULE 16. The Putting Green

16.0 DEFINED TERMS. This rule contains the following defined terms:
- addressing the ball (35.2);
- hole (35.22);
- hole out (35.23);
- line of putt (35.27);
- loose impediment (35.28);
- movable obstruction (35.33(B));
- move (35.30);
- penalty stroke (35.38);
- putting green (35.40);
- stipulated round (35.46); and
- stroke (35.47).

16.1 GENERAL

(A) No Touching Line of Putt. You must not touch the line of putt, except when:

(1) removing loose impediments without pressing anything down;

(2) addressing the ball — that is, you may place your club in front of the ball without pressing anything down;

(3) measuring (Rule 18.6);

(4) lifting or re-placing the ball (Rule 16.1(B));

(5) pressing down a ball marker;

(6) repairing old hole plugs or ball marks on the putting green (Rule 16.1(C)); and

(7) removing movable obstructions (Rule 24.1).

(B) Lifting Ball. A ball on the putting green may be marked, lifted, cleaned, and re-placed. But if your ball might affect another ball's movement, you can't lift your ball while that ball is in motion.

(C) Repairing Hole Plugs, Ball Marks, and Other Damage. You may repair an old hole plug or damage to the putting green caused by any ball, whether or not your ball lies on the putting green. If you accidentally move a ball or ball marker while making this repair, the ball or marker must be re-placed. There is no penalty if the movement of the ball or ball marker is directly caused by the specific act of repairing an old hole plug or damage to the putting green caused by a ball. Otherwise, you receive a penalty stroke under Rule 18.2(A). Any other damage to the putting green (such as spike marks) must not be repaired if doing so might help you in your play of the hole.

(D) No Testing of Surface. During the stipulated round, you must not test any putting green by rolling a ball or scraping the surface. But between play of two holes you may practice as allowed by Rule 7.2.

(E) No Standing Astride or on Line of Putt. You must not make a stroke on the putting green with either foot touching or while straddling the line of putt or an extension of that line behind the ball. If you accidentally violate this Rule when trying to avoid standing on another player's line of putt, there is no penalty.

(F) Making Stroke While Another Ball Is in Motion. You must not make a stroke while another ball is in motion after a stroke from the putting green. But there is no penalty if it was your turn to play.

(G) Penalty. If you violate this Rule 16.1, you lose the hole in match play or receive a two-stroke penalty in stroke play.

16.2 BALL OVERHANGING HOLE

(A) Status of the Ball. When any part of the ball overhangs the edge of the hole, you're allowed time to reach the hole without unreasonable delay and an additional ten seconds to determine whether the ball is at rest. If by then the ball has not fallen into the hole, it is considered to be at rest and play must continue.

(B) Determining Score for the Hole. If the ball falls into the hole before the ten seconds expire, you're considered to have holed out with your last stroke. If the ball falls into the hole after the ten seconds expire, you're considered to have holed out with your last stroke, but you must also add a penalty stroke to your score for the hole.

RULE 17. The Flagstick

17.0 DEFINED TERMS. This rule contains the following defined terms:
- caddie (35.7);
- course (35.13);

- flagstick (35.15);
- hole (35.22);
- hole out (35.23);
- move (35.30);
- putting green (35.40);
- referee (35.41); and
- stroke (35.47).

17.1 FLAGSTICK ATTENDED, HELD UP, OR REMOVED

(A) What Is Allowed. Before a stroke made from anywhere on the course, you may have someone (other than a referee) attend the flagstick, hold it up, or remove it to indicate the position of the hole. Removing an unattended flagstick during or after the stroke is not allowed if it might affect a ball's movement.

(B) Authorized Attendance. If the flagstick is attended, held up, or removed by anyone before your stroke with your knowledge and you don't object, you're considered to have authorized that conduct. If anyone attends or holds up the flagstick or stands near the hole while a stroke is being made, that person is considered to be attending the flagstick until the ball comes to rest.

(C) Penalty. If you violate this Rule 17.1, you lose the hole in match play or receive a two-stroke penalty in stroke play.

17.2 UNAUTHORIZED ATTENDANCE

(A) Restriction. If it might affect a ball's movement, you or your caddie must not attend, hold up, or remove the flagstick without authority while another player is making a stroke or another player's ball is in motion.

(B) Penalty. If this Rule 17.2 is violated, the player attending the flagstick without authority loses the hole in match play or receives a two-stroke penalty in stroke play.

17.3 BALL STRIKING FLAGSTICK OR ATTENDANT

(A) General Rule. If your ball strikes any of the following, you lose the hole in match play or receive a two-stroke penalty in stroke play and the ball is played as it lies:

(1) the flagstick when attended, removed, or held up by any person with your authority;

(2) any person attending or holding up the flagstick with your authority or anything carried by that person; or

(3) the flagstick in the hole, unattended, when your ball has been played from the putting green.

(B) Stroke Play: Flagstick Struck During Unauthorized Attendance. In stroke play, if your ball strikes a flagstick or the person attending it when that person has no authority to attend it, you aren't penalized and the ball is played as it lies. But if the ball was played from the putting green, your stroke is canceled and you must replay it. If your ball isn't re-placed and replayed, you receive a two-stroke penalty..

17.4 BALL RESTING AGAINST FLAGSTICK. When the flagstick is in the hole and your ball rests against it, you or a person you authorize may move the flagstick. If the ball falls into the hole, you are considered to have holed out with your previous stroke. If the ball moves but is not holed, it must be placed on the lip of the hole without penalty.

RULE 18. Movement of Ball at Rest

18.0 DEFINED TERMS. This rule contains the following defined terms:
- abnormal ground condition (35.1);
- addressing the ball (35.2);
- ball in play (35.4);
- caddie (35.7);
- equipment (35.14);
- fellow-competitor (35.12(B), (C));
- hazard (35.21);
- hole (35.22);
- loose impediment (35.28);
- movable obstruction (35.33(B));
- move (35.30);
- opponent (35.34);
- outside agency (35.36);
- partner (35.37);
- penalty stroke (35.38);
- putting green (35.40);
- rules (35.42);
- stroke (35.47); and
- water hazard (35.52).

18.1 BALL MOVED BY AN OUTSIDE AGENCY. If a ball at rest is moved by an outside agency, there is no penalty and the ball must be re-placed. You may apply this Rule 18.1 if you cannot find your ball and you know or are almost certain that it was moved by an outside agency. Otherwise, your ball is considered lost and you must proceed under Rule 27.1 (stroke and distance). For a ball at rest moved by another ball, see Rule 18.5.

18.2 BALL MOVED BY PLAYER, PARTNER, CADDIE, OR EQUIPMENT

(A) General Restriction. You, your partner, and either of your caddies must not touch or move your ball in play, except as the rules say otherwise.

(B) Penalty. If you, your partner, either of your caddies, or the equipment of you or your partner lifts or moves the ball, touches it purposely, or causes your ball to move except as specifically allowed by a rule, you receive a penalty stroke. The ball must be re-placed unless the movement of the ball occurs after you have begun the backward movement of the club for the stroke and you do not discontinue your stroke.

(C) Exceptions. While you're addressing the ball before a stroke, there is no penalty if your club touches the ball but doesn't move it. And there is no penalty if you accidentally cause your ball to move in the following circumstances:

(1) measuring (for example, to determine which ball is farther from the hole) (Rule 18.6);

(2) searching for a ball covered by sand or re-creating the lie of a ball that has been altered during a search; searching for a ball in an obstruction or an abnormal ground condition; replacing loose impediments moved in a water hazard while finding or identifying a ball; or probing for a ball in water in a water hazard (Rule 12.1);

(3) repairing a hole plug or ball mark on the putting green (Rule 16.1(C));

(4) removing loose impediments on the putting green (Rule 23.2(B));

(5) lifting a ball under a rule (Rule 20.1(C)(1));

(6) placing or re-placing a ball under a rule (Rule 20.3(A)); and

(7) removing a movable obstruction (Rule 24.1(A)(2)).

18.3 BALL MOVED BY OPPONENT, CADDIE, OR EQUIPMENT IN MATCH PLAY

(A) During Search for the Ball. During a search for your ball, if an opponent or the opponent's caddie or equipment touches or moves the ball, there is no penalty. The ball must be re-placed.

(B) Other Than During Search. At any other time, if your ball is touched or moved by an opponent or the opponent's caddie or equipment, except as the rules provide, the opponent receives a penalty stroke. The ball must be re-placed.

18.4 BALL MOVED BY A FELLOW-COMPETITOR, CADDIE, OR EQUIPMENT IN STROKE PLAY.

If your ball is touched or moved by a fellow-competitor or a fellow-competitor's caddie or equipment, there is no penalty (same as Rule 18.1). The ball must be re-placed.

18.5 BALL MOVED BY ANOTHER BALL.

If a ball in play and at rest is moved by another ball put in motion by a stroke, the moved ball must be re-placed, and the striking ball is played as it lies (see Rule 19.5(A)).

18.6 BALL MOVED IN MEASURING.

If you move a ball or ball marker in measuring while proceeding under a rule, the ball or ball marker must be re-placed. There is no penalty if the movement of the ball or ball marker is directly caused by the specific act of measuring. Otherwise, you receive a penalty stroke under Rule 18.2(A).

18.7 PROCEDURES AND PENALTIES

(A) Procedures. If a ball to be re-placed under Rule 18 is not immediately recoverable, another ball may be substituted. If it is impossible to determine where a ball is to be placed or re-placed, see Rule 20.3(B). If the original lie of a ball to be placed or re-placed has been altered, see Rule 20.3(C).

(B) Penalty. If you violate this Rule 18, you lose the hole in match play or receive a two-stroke penalty in stroke play. If you fail to re-place a ball when required or make a stroke at an improperly substituted ball, you receive this general penalty for violating Rule 18, but no additional penalty is applied.

RULE 19.
Moving Ball Deflected or Stopped

19.0 DEFINED TERMS. This rule contains the following defined terms:

- ball in play (35.4);
- caddie (35.7);
- equipment (35.14);
- fellow-competitor (35.12(B), (C));
- flagstick (35.15);
- hazard (35.21);
- hole (35.22);
- opponent (35.34);
- outside agency (35.36);
- partner (35.37);
- putting green (35.40);
- stroke (35.47); and
- through the green (35.51).

19.1 BY OUTSIDE AGENCY

(A) General. If your ball in motion is accidentally deflected or stopped by an outside agency, there is no penalty and you must play the ball as it lies. If the ball is not immediately recoverable, you may substitute another ball.

(B) Exceptions for Moving or Animate Outside Agencies

(1) Ball Anywhere Other Than Putting Green. If you play your ball from anywhere except the putting green and it comes to rest on a moving or animate outside agency, you must return your ball as near as possible to the spot where the outside agency was when the ball came to rest on it (see Rule 20.3(B) for correct procedures).

(2) Ball on Putting Green. If you play your ball from the putting green and it is deflected or stopped by a moving or animate outside agency (except a worm, insect, or the like)—or stops on such an agency—the stroke is canceled and replayed.

(C) Procedures When Purposely Deflected. If your ball has been purposely deflected or stopped by an outside agency, the following procedures apply:

(1) Stroke from Anywhere Other Than Putting Green. You must estimate where the ball would have come to rest. If that spot is:

(a) through the green or in a hazard, you must drop the ball as near as possible to the estimated spot;

(b) out of bounds, you must proceed under Rule 27.1;

(c) on the putting green, you must place the ball on the estimated spot.

(2) Stroke from Putting Green. Your stroke is canceled and the ball must be re-placed and re-played.

(3) Particular Outside Agencies. If the outside agency is a fellow-competitor or a fellow-competitor's caddie, Rule 1.2 applies to the fellow-competitor.

(D) Flagstick Exception. This Rule 19.1 does not apply if the ball is deflected or stopped by a person attending or holding up the flagstick or by anything carried by that person (see Rule 17.3(B)).

19.2 BY PLAYER, PARTNER, CADDIE, OR EQUIPMENT

(A) General Rule. If you, your partner, or either of your caddies or equipment accidentally deflects or stops your ball, you receive a one-stroke penalty and the ball is played as it lies. If the deflected ball comes to rest in or on your, your partner's, or either of your caddies' clothes or equipment, you must proceed as follows: Through the green or in a hazard, drop the ball — or on a putting green place the ball — as near as possible to where the item was when your ball came to rest in or on it.

(B) Dropped Ball Exception. This Rule 19.2 does not apply if you are using the drop procedures in Rule 20.2 (see Rule 20.2(A)(3)).

(C) Flagstick Exception. This Rule 19.2 does not apply if the ball is deflected or stopped by a person attending or holding up the flagstick or by anything carried by that person (see Rule 17.3(B)).

19.3 BY OPPONENT, CADDIE, OR EQUIPMENT IN MATCH PLAY

(A) General Rule. If your opponent or the opponent's caddie or equipment accidentally deflects or stops your ball, there is no penalty.

(B) Options and Procedures. Proceed as follows:
(1) Before either side makes another stroke, you

may cancel the stroke and play a ball from the spot where you played the original ball (see Rule 20.5); or

(2) You may play the ball as it lies. But if your ball comes to rest in or on your opponent's or his or her caddie's clothes or equipment, then do this: through the green or in a hazard, drop the ball — or, on a putting green, place the ball — as near as possible to where the item was when your ball came to rest in or on it.

(c) Flagstick Exception. This Rule 19.3 does not apply if the ball is deflected or stopped by a person attending or holding up the flagstick or by anything carried by that person (see Rule 17.3(B)).

19.4 BY FELLOW-COMPETITOR, CADDIE, OR EQUIPMENT IN STROKE PLAY.

In stroke play, if your ball is deflected or stopped by a fellow-competitor, or a fellow-competitor's caddie or equipment, Rule 19.1 applies. This Rule 19.4 does not apply if the ball is deflected or stopped by a person attending or holding up the flagstick or by anything carried by that person (see Rule 17.3(B)).

19.5 BY ANOTHER BALL

(A) At Rest. If your ball in motion after a stroke is deflected or stopped by a ball in play and at rest, there is no penalty. Play the ball as it lies. But in stroke play, you are penalized two strokes if both balls were on the putting green before the stroke.

(B) In Motion. If your ball is deflected or stopped by another ball in motion after a stroke, there is no penalty. Play the ball as it lies. But there are two exceptions:

(1) Penalty Exceptions. If you hit out of turn, violating Rule 10.1 or 16.1(F), that specific rule applies; and

(2) Replay Exception. If your ball was on the putting green before the stroke, the stroke is canceled and replayed (Rule 19.1(B)(2)).

19.6 PENALTY. If you violate this Rule 19, you lose the hole in match play or receive a two-stroke penalty in stroke play.

RULE 20.
Procedures for Lifting, Dropping, and Placing; Playing from Wrong Place

20.0 DEFINED TERMS. This rule contains the following defined terms:
- abnormal ground condition (35.1);
- ball in play (35.4);
- bunker (35.6);
- caddie (35.7);
- Committee (35.11);
- course (35.13);
- equipment (35.14);
- hazard (35.21);
- hole (35.22);
- immovable obstruction (35.33);
- lateral water hazard (35.25);
- move (35.30);
- nearest point of relief (35.31);
- out of bounds (35.35);
- partner (35.37);

- penalty stroke (35.38);
- putting green (35.40);
- rule (35.42);
- stance (35.45);
- stroke (35.47);
- substituted ball (35.48);
- teeing ground (35.50);
- through the green (35.51);
- water hazard (35.52); and
- wrong putting green (35.54).

20.1 MARKING AND LIFTING THE BALL

(A) Who May Lift. A ball to be lifted under the rules may be lifted by you, your partner, or another person that you've authorized. You remain responsible for any rule violations during this process.

(B) How to Mark and Lift

(1) Procedure. Your ball's position must be marked before it is lifted under any rule that requires re-placement. If it is not marked, you receive a one-stroke penalty and the ball must be re-placed. If it is not re-placed, you receive the general penalty for violating this Rule 20.1, but no further penalties are applied under this rule.

(2) Ball Marker. The position of a ball to be lifted should be marked by placing a ball marker, a small coin, or other similar object immediately behind the ball. If the ball marker interferes with the play, stance, or stroke of another player, it should be placed one or more clubhead-lengths to one side.

(C) Exceptions

(1) If a ball or ball marker is accidentally moved when you lift the ball or mark its position, the ball or the ball marker must be re-placed. There is no penalty if the movement of the ball or ball marker is directly caused by the specific act of marking the ball's position or lifting it. Otherwise, you receive a penalty stroke under this rule or Rule 18.2(A).

(2) This rule does not apply if you have received a penalty for violating Rule 5.3 or 12.2.

20.2 DROPPING AND RE-DROPPING THE BALL

(A) Procedure

(1) By Whom and How. If you're allowed to drop a ball under the rules, you must drop it yourself. You must stand erect, hold the ball at shoulder height and at arm's length, and drop it. If a ball is dropped by anyone else or in any other manner and the error is not corrected as described in Rule 20.6, you receive a penalty stroke.

(2) Striking the Course. A dropped ball must first strike a part of the course where the applicable rule requires the ball to be dropped. If it doesn't, Rules 20.6 (correcting an improper drop) and 20.7 (playing from a wrong place) apply.

(3) Invalid Drop. If a dropped ball touches any person or any player's equipment before or after it strikes a part of the course and before it comes to rest, the ball must be re-dropped without penalty. There is no limit to the number of times a ball can be re-dropped under these circumstances.

(B) Where to Drop.
When a ball is to be dropped as near as possible to a specific spot, it cannot be dropped nearer the hole than that spot. If you don't know the specific spot, the location for dropping the ball should be estimated.

(C) When to Re-drop

(1) A ball dropped properly according to Rule 20.2(A) must be re-dropped without penalty if it:

(a) rolls into and stops in a hazard;

(b) rolls out of and stops outside a hazard;

(c) rolls onto and stops on a putting green;

(d) rolls and stops out of bounds;

(e) rolls to and stops in a position where there is interference by the condition from which relief was taken (as in the conditions specified in Rule 24.2 (immovable obstruction); Rule 25.1 (abnormal ground condition); Rule 25.4 (wrong putting green); Rule 33.1(c) (a local rule for an abnormal condition); or Rule 25.3 (a ball's own pitch-mark));

(f) rolls and stops more than two club-lengths from where it first struck a part of the course; or

(g) rolls and stops closer to the hole than:

> (i) its original or estimated position (see Rule 20.2(B)), unless the rules permit otherwise;
>
> (ii) the nearest point of relief or maximum available relief (Rule 24.2, 25.1, or 25.4); or
>
> (iii) the point where the original ball last crossed the margin of the water hazard or lateral water hazard (Rule 26.1(B)(2)).

(2) Place After Two Tries. If on the second drop attempt a ball rolls into any position listed above, it must be placed as near as possible to the spot where it first struck a part of the course on the second drop.

(3) Other Procedures

(a) If a ball to be re-dropped or placed under this rule is not immediately recoverable, another ball may be substituted.

(b) If a ball when dropped or re-dropped comes to rest and later moves, the ball is played as it lies (unless any other rule applies).

20.3 PLACING OR RETURNING THE BALL

(A) By Whom

(1) Responsibility. If you're to place a ball under the rules, either you or your partner may place it. If a ball is to be re-placed, either you, your partner, or the person who lifted or moved the ball must return it to its previous location. But you remain responsible for any rule violations. The person who lifted or moved the ball does not have to be the same person who re-places the ball.

(2) Penalty. If your ball is placed or re-placed by an unauthorized person and you don't correct the error as allowed by Rule 20.6, you receive a one-stroke penalty. If your ball is placed or re-placed somewhere other than on the spot from where it was lifted or moved, and you don't correct the error as allowed by Rule 20.6, you lose the hole in match play or receive a two-stroke penalty in stroke play.

(3) Exception. If a ball or ball marker is accidentally moved while you're placing or re-placing the ball, the ball or ball marker must be re-placed. There is no penalty if the movement of the ball or ball marker is directly caused by the specific act of placing or re-placing the ball or removing the ball marker. Otherwise, you are penalized one stroke under Rule 18.2(A) or Rule 20.1.

(B) Where to Place; Spot Not Known

(1) Where. A ball to be placed or re-placed must be returned to the spot from which it was lifted or moved.

(2) Spot Not Known. If it is impossible to determine the specific spot where the ball is to be placed or re-placed, you must proceed as follows:

(a) through the green, drop the ball as near as possible to its original position, but not in a hazard or on a putting green;

(b) in a hazard, drop the ball in the hazard as near as possible to its original position; or

(c) on the putting green, place the ball as near as possible to its original position, but not in a hazard.

(d) **Exception.** This Rule 20.3(B)(2) doesn't apply when resuming play under Rule 6.8(D) and you don't know the precise spot to re-place your ball.

(c) **When the Original Lie Is Altered.** If the original lie of a ball to be re-placed has been altered, you must proceed as follows:

(1) **Generally.** Except in a hazard, place the ball in the nearest lie most similar to the original lie not more than one club-length from the original lie, but not nearer the hole and not in a hazard.

(2) **Water Hazard.** In a water hazard, place the ball in the water hazard in the nearest lie most similar to the original lie not more than one club-length from the original lie, but not nearer the hole.

(3) **Bunker.** In a bunker, place the ball in the best possible re-creation of the original lie.

(4) **Procedural Note.** If the original lie of a ball to be placed or re-placed is altered and it is impossible to determine the exact spot to return the ball, follow these procedures: if the nature of the original lie is known, Rule 20.3(C) applies; otherwise, Rule 20.3(B) applies.

(5) **Exception.** If you are searching for or identifying a ball covered by sand, see Rule 12.1(B).

(D) **When the Ball Won't Come to Rest on the Spot.** If a placed ball will not come to rest on the spot where it was placed, it is re-placed without penalty. If it still fails to come to rest on that spot, you must proceed as follows:

(1) Generally. Except in a hazard, place it at the nearest spot where it can remain at rest but is not nearer the hole and not in a hazard.

(2) Hazard. In a hazard, place it in the hazard at the nearest spot where it can remain at rest but is not nearer the hole.

(3) Placed Ball Moves. If a placed ball comes to rest, and it later moves, play the ball as it lies without penalty (unless some other rule applies).

(E) **Penalty.** If you violate Rule 20.1, Rule 20.2, or Rule 20.3, you lose the hole in match play or receive a two-stroke penalty in stroke play. When using these rules, if you make a stroke at an improperly substituted ball (see Rule 15.1), you lose the hole in match play or receive a two-stroke penalty in stroke play, but no other penalty under these rules. If you play from a wrong place, see Rule 20.7.

20.4 WHEN BALL IS IN PLAY

(A) **Status.** A lifted ball regains status as a ball in play when it is dropped or placed. A substituted ball becomes the ball in play when it has been dropped or placed. (Note: A ball that has been re-placed is in play whether or not the ball marker has been removed. A ball is "in play" when it leaves your hand, not when it comes to rest.)

(B) **Penalty.** The penalty for a ball incorrectly substituted is specified in Rule 15.1(B). The correction procedure for a ball wrongly substituted, dropped, or placed appears in Rule 20.6.

20.5 PLAYING NEXT STROKE FROM WHERE PREVIOUS STROKE PLAYED

(A) **Procedure.** If you choose to make or are required to make your next stroke from the place where a previous stroke was made, you must proceed as follows:

(1) if the stroke is to be made from the teeing ground, you may play the ball from anywhere within the teeing ground and it may be teed;

(2) if the stroke is to be made from anywhere through the green or from a hazard, drop the ball (see Rule 20.2(A)(2)); or

(3) if the stroke is to be made on the putting green, place the ball on the putting green.

(B) Penalty. If you violate this Rule 20.5, you lose the hole in match play or receive a two-stroke penalty in stroke play.

20.6 LIFTING BALL INCORRECTLY SUBSTITUTED, DROPPED, OR PLACED.

If you substitute, drop, or place a ball in a wrong place or otherwise not according to the rules, you may lift it without penalty before playing. You may then proceed correctly.

20.7 PLAYING FROM WRONG PLACE

(A) Generally

(1) Wrong Place. You're considered to have played from a wrong place if you make a stroke at your ball in play in the following circumstances:

(a) on a part of the course where the rules don't permit a stroke to be made or a ball to be dropped or placed; or

(b) when the rules require a dropped ball to be re-dropped (see Rule 20.2(C)) or a moved ball to be re-placed (see Rule 18).

(2) Teeing Ground. If you play a ball from outside the teeing ground or from a wrong teeing ground, Rules 11.4 and 11.5 apply.

(B) Match Play. If you make a stroke from a wrong place, you lose the hole.

(c) Stroke Play

(1) General Rule. If you make a stroke from a wrong place, you should play out the hole with that ball, as long as a serious violation has not occurred. You'll receive the penalty prescribed by the applicable rule (for example, if you drop a ball in a wrong place when taking relief from a water hazard, you receive a two-stroke penalty in stroke play).

(2) Penalty Exceptions. If you receive a penalty for making a stroke from a wrong place, there is no additional penalty for:

(a) playing an improperly substituted ball;

(b) dropping a ball when the rules require it to be placed, or placing a ball when the rules require it to be dropped;

(c) dropping a ball incorrectly (see Rule 20.2(A)); or

(d) having a ball put into play by a person not allowed to do so under the rules.

(3) Correction Procedures for a Serious Violation

(a) **Serious Violation.** You've committed a serious violation of the applicable rule if the Committee considers that you gained a significant advantage by playing from a wrong place.

(b) **Procedures.** If you play from a wrong place and believe that a serious violation may be involved, invoke the following corrective procedures. If you have not made a stroke from the next teeing ground or, if the hole being played is the last hole of the round and you have not left the putting green, declare that you will play out the hole with a second ball played according to the rules. If a serious violation has occurred and you don't correct it, you're disqualified.

(c) **Determining Score for the Hole.** If you play a second ball, you must report these actions to the Committee before returning your scorecard. If you don't, you're disqualified. The Committee decides whether you seriously violated the applicable rule. If so, the score with the second ball counts, and you'll have a two-stroke penalty added to your score with that ball. If you play a second ball, and it is ruled not to count, penalty strokes incurred solely by playing the ball that does not count, and any strokes later taken with that ball, are disregarded.

RULE 21. Cleaning Your Ball

21.0 DEFINED TERM. This rule contains the following defined term:

- ball unfit for play (35.5)

21.1 GENERAL RULE. You may clean a ball when lifting it except when it has been lifted:

(A) to determine whether it is unfit for play (Rule 5.3);

(B) for identification (Rule 12.2), in which case it may be cleaned only to the extent necessary for identification; or

(C) because it is interfering with or assisting play (Rule 22).

21.2 PENALTY AND PROCEDURES

(A) If you clean your ball when you're not allowed to, you receive a one-stroke penalty. And if you've lifted the ball, it must be re-placed.

(B) If you are required to re-place your ball and don't, you receive the general penalty for violating the procedures specified in Rule 20.3(A), but no additional penalty under this Rule 21.

21.3 PENALTY LIMITS. If you receive a penalty for not following Rule 5.3, 12.2, or 22, no additional penalty under this Rule 21 is applied.

RULE 22.
Ball Interfering with or Assisting Play

22.0 DEFINED TERMS. This rule contains the following defined terms:
- hole (35.22);
- putting green (35.40); and
- stroke (35.47).

22.1 GENERAL RULE. You may lift your ball if, as it lies, it might help any other player. You may have any ball lifted if the ball might interfere with your play or help someone else's play. A ball lifted under this rule is re-placed.

22.2 EXCEPTIONS
(A) If your ball might affect a ball's movement, you can't lift your ball while another one is in motion.
(B) In stroke play only, if you're required to lift your ball, you may play first rather than lift.
(C) Except on the putting green, you may not lift your ball solely because you believe that it might interfere with the play of another player.

22.3 NO CLEANING. Except on the putting green, the ball may not be cleaned when lifted under this rule (see Rule 21).

22.4 PENALTIES

(A) If you violate this Rule 22, you lose the hole in match play or receive a two-stroke penalty in stroke play.

(B) Off the putting green, if you lift your ball because you think it interferes, without being asked to do so, you receive a one-stroke penalty for violating Rule 18.2, but no further penalty under this Rule 22.

(C) In stroke play, if the Committee determines that competitors have agreed not to lift a ball that might help a competitor, they are disqualified.

RULE 23. Loose Impediments

23.0 DEFINED TERMS. This rule contains the following defined terms:
- caddie (35.7);
- hazard (35.21);
- hole (35.22);
- loose impediments (35.28)
- move (35.30);
- partner (35.37);
- penalty stroke (35.38); and
- putting green (35.40).

23.1 GENERAL RULE. You may remove any loose impediment without penalty, unless the ball and the loose impediment touch the same hazard. If the ball moves during this process, see Rule 23.2.

23.2 BALL MOVING AFTER A LOOSE IMPEDIMENT IS TOUCHED

(A) Ball Anywhere but the Putting Green. If a loose impediment is moved by you, your partner, or either of your caddies and this causes your ball to move, you receive a one-stroke penalty under Rule 18.2. The ball must be re-placed.

(B) Ball on the Putting Green. If you accidentally move your ball or your ball marker while removing a loose impediment on the putting green, the ball or marker must be re-placed. There is no penalty if the movement of the ball or the ball marker resulted directly from the removal of the loose impediment. Otherwise, you receive a penalty stroke under Rule 18.2.

23.3 EXCEPTION. When a ball is in motion, a loose impediment that might affect a ball's movement must not be removed.

23.4 PENALTY. If you violate this Rule 23, you lose the hole in match play or receive a two-stroke penalty in stroke play.

RULE 24.
Interference and Relief from Obstructions

24.0 DEFINED TERMS. This rule contains the following defined terms:
- bunker (35.6);
- Committee (35.11);

- equipment (35.14);
- flagstick (35.15);
- hazard (35.21);
- hole (35.22);
- immovable obstructions (35.33);
- lateral water hazard (35.25);
- line of play (35.26);
- line of putt (35.27);
- lost ball (35.29);
- movable obstructions (35.33(B));
- move (35.30);
- nearest point of relief (35.31);
- obstruction (35.33);
- putting green (35.40);
- rule (35.42);
- stance (35.45);
- stroke (35.47);
- teeing ground (35.50);
- through the green (35.51); and
- water hazard (35.52).

24.1 MOVABLE OBSTRUCTIONS

(A) Relief Procedures

(1) In General. You may obtain relief without penalty from a movable obstruction.

(2) Ball Not in or on Obstruction. If the ball does not lie in or on the obstruction, you may remove the obstruction. If the ball moves, it must be re-placed, and there is no penalty if the movement of the ball is directly caused by the removal of the obstruction. Otherwise, Rule 18.2(A) applies.

(3) Ball in or on Obstruction. If the ball lies in or on the obstruction, you may lift the ball without penalty and remove the obstruction. The ball is put back in play by returning it as near as possible to the spot directly under the place where the ball lay in or on the obstruction but not nearer the hole. Through the green or in a hazard, the ball is dropped; on the putting green, it is placed.

(B) Exception. When a ball is in motion, an obstruction that might affect a ball's movement must not be removed. But you may remove any player's equipment or a flagstick that is attended, held up, or removed.

(C) Procedural Reminders

(1) Substituting Ball. If a ball to be dropped or placed under this rule is not immediately recoverable, you may substitute another ball.

(2) Cleaning Your Ball. You may clean the ball when lifting under this Rule 24.1(A).

24.2 IMMOVABLE OBSTRUCTIONS

(A) Interference Defined. Interference by an immovable obstruction occurs when your ball lies in or on an obstruction, or so close that the obstruction interferes with your stance or your intended swing. If your ball lies on the putting green, interference also occurs if an immovable obstruction on the putting green intervenes on your line of putt. Otherwise, hindrance with the line of play is not interference under this rule.

(B) Relief Procedures. You may obtain relief without penalty from interference by an immovable obstruction as follows.

(1) Through the Green. If the ball lies through the green, determine the nearest point of relief that is not in a hazard or on a putting green. Then lift the ball and drop it within one club-length of the nearest point of relief, but not nearer the hole and not in a hazard or on a putting green.

(2) In a Bunker. If the ball is in a bunker, you must lift and drop the ball either:

(a) without a penalty, according to (B)(1), except that the nearest point of relief must be in the bunker and the ball must be dropped in the bunker; or

(b) under penalty of one stroke, outside the bunker, keeping the point where the ball lay directly between the hole and the spot where the ball is dropped, with no limit on how far behind the bunker the ball may be dropped.

(3) On the Putting Green. If the ball lies on the putting green, lift the ball and place it at the nearest point of relief not in a hazard and not nearer the hole. The nearest point of relief may be off the putting green.

(4) On the Teeing Ground. If the ball lies on the teeing ground, you must lift the ball and drop it according to Rule 24.2(B)(1).

(5) Cleaning Your Ball. You may clean the ball when lifting under this Rule 24.2(B).

(c) Exceptions

(1) Water Hazard. If the ball is in a water hazard or lateral water hazard, you can't receive relief without penalty from interference by an immovable obstruction. You must play the ball as it lies or proceed under Rule 26.1.

(2) Unreasonable Situation. You can't receive relief without penalty under Rule 24.2(B) if:

(a) it is clearly unreasonable for you to make a stroke because of interference by anything other than an immovable obstruction; or

(b) interference by an immovable obstruction would occur only by using a clearly unreasonable stroke, stance, swing, or direction of play.

(D) Miscellaneous Procedures

(1) Substituting Ball. If a ball to be dropped or placed under this rule is not immediately recoverable, you may substitute another ball.

(2) Committee Restriction. The Committee may make a local rule stating that the player must determine the nearest point of relief without crossing over, through, or under the obstruction.

24.3 BALL NOT FOUND IN AN OBSTRUCTION

(A) Status of Ball. If you cannot find your ball and you know or are almost certain that it is lost in an obstruction, then you may apply this Rule 24.3. Otherwise, your ball is considered lost outside the obstruction and you must proceed under Rule 27.1 (stroke and distance).

(B) Relief Procedures: Movable Obstruction. If a ball is lost in a movable obstruction, you may remove the obstruction without penalty. The ball is put back into play by returning it as near as possible to the spot directly under the place where the ball last entered the obstruction but not nearer the hole. Through the green or in a hazard, the ball is dropped; on the putting green, it is placed.

(C) Relief Procedures: Immovable Obstruction. If a ball is lost in an immovable obstruction, the spot where the ball last entered the obstruction is determined, and for purposes of applying this rule the ball is considered to lie at that spot. You must then proceed as follows:

(1) Through the Green. If the ball last entered the immovable obstruction at a spot through the green, you may substitute another ball without penalty and take relief as prescribed in Rule 24.2(B)(1).

(2) In a Bunker. If the ball last entered the immovable obstruction at a spot in a bunker, you may substitute another ball without penalty and take relief as prescribed in Rule 24.2(B)(2).

(3) On the Putting Green. If the ball last entered the immovable obstruction at a spot on the putting green, you may substitute another ball without penalty and take relief as prescribed in Rule 24.2(B)(3).

(4) In a Water Hazard. If the ball last entered the immovable obstruction at a spot in a water hazard or lateral water hazard, you don't get relief without penalty. You must proceed under Rule 26.1.

(D) **Penalty.** If you violate this Rule 24, you lose the hole in match play or receive a two-stroke penalty in stroke play.

RULE 25.
Interference and Relief from Abnormal Ground Conditions, Embedded Ball, or Wrong Putting Green

25.0 DEFINED TERMS. This rule contains the following defined terms:

- abnormal ground condition (35.1);
- bunker (35.6);
- closely mown area (35.9);

- Committee (35.11);
- course (35.13);
- hazard (35.21);
- hole (35.22);
- lateral water hazard (35.25);
- line of play (35.26);
- line of putt (35.27);
- local rule (35.42(c));
- lost ball (35.29);
- nearest point of relief (35.31);
- putting green (35.40);
- stance (35.45);
- stroke (35.47);
- teeing ground (35.50);
- through the green (35.51);
- water hazard (35.52); and
- wrong putting green (35.54).

25.1 ABNORMAL GROUND CONDITION
(A) Interference Defined
(1) General. Interference by an abnormal ground condition occurs when your ball lies in the condition or when the condition interferes with your stance or the area of your intended swing. If your ball lies on the putting green, interference also occurs if the condition on the putting green intervenes on your line of putt. Otherwise, hindrance with the line of play is not interference under this rule.

(2) Exception. The Committee may make a local rule denying relief from an abnormal ground condition that interferes only with a player's stance (such as seams of new sod).

(B) Relief Procedures. You may obtain relief without

penalty from interference by an abnormal ground condition as follows:

(1) Through the Green. If the ball lies through the green, determine the nearest point of relief that is not in a hazard or on a putting green. Lift the ball and drop it within one club-length of the nearest point of relief not nearer the hole. You must drop the ball on a part of the course that completely avoids interference from the condition.

(2) In a Bunker. If the ball is in a bunker, you must lift and drop the ball either:

(a) without penalty, according to (B)(I), with these qualifications:

> (i) the nearest point of relief must be in the bunker and the ball must be dropped in the bunker; and
>
> (ii) if complete relief is impossible, the ball may be dropped in the bunker as near as possible to the spot where the ball lay, but not nearer the hole, on a part of the course that gives maximum available relief from the condition;

or

(b) under penalty of one stroke, outside the bunker, keeping the point where the ball lay directly between the hole and the spot where the ball is dropped, with no limit on how far behind the bunker the ball may be dropped.

(3) On the Putting Green. If the ball lies on the putting green, you must lift the ball and place it without penalty at the nearest point of relief that is not in a hazard. If complete relief is impossible, the ball may be placed as near as possible to where it lay with maximum available relief from the condition, but not nearer the hole or in a hazard. The nearest point of relief or maximum available relief may be off the putting green.

(4) On the Teeing Ground. If the ball lies on the teeing ground, you must lift it and drop it according to Rule 25.1(B)(1).

(c) Exceptions

(1) Water Hazard. If a ball is in a water hazard or lateral water hazard, you can't receive relief without penalty from interference by an abnormal ground condition. You must either play the ball as it lies, unless prohibited by a local rule, or proceed under Rule 26.1.

(2) Unreasonable Situation. You can't receive relief without penalty under Rule 25.1(B) if:

(a) it is clearly unreasonable for you to make a stroke because of interference by anything other than a condition covered by Rule 25.1(A); or

(b) interference by the condition would occur only by using a clearly unreasonable stroke, stance, swing, or direction of play.

(D) Procedural Reminders

(1) Substituting Ball. If a ball to be dropped or placed under this rule is not immediately recoverable, you may substitute another ball.

(2) Cleaning Ball. You may clean the ball when lifting under this Rule 25.1.

25.2 BALL NOT FOUND IN ABNORMAL GROUND CONDITION

(A) Status of Ball. If you cannot find your ball and you know or are almost certain that it is lost in an abnormal ground condition, then you may apply this Rule 25.2. Otherwise, your ball is considered lost outside the abnormal ground condition and you must proceed under Rule 27.1 (stroke and distance).

(B) Relief Procedures. If a ball is lost in an abnormal ground condition, the spot where the ball last entered the condition is determined, and for purposes of applying this rule the ball is considered to lie at that spot. You must then proceed as follows:

(1) Through the Green. If the ball last entered the abnormal ground condition at a spot through the green, you may substitute another ball without penalty and take relief as prescribed in Rule 25.1(B)(1).

(2) In a Bunker. If the ball last entered the abnormal ground condition at a spot in a bunker, you may substitute another ball without penalty and take relief as prescribed in Rule 25.1(B)(2).

(3) On the Putting Green. If the ball last entered the abnormal ground condition at a spot on the putting green, you may substitute another ball without penalty and take relief as prescribed in Rule 25.1(B)(3).

(4) In a Water Hazard. If the ball last entered the abnormal condition at a spot in a water hazard, you don't get relief without penalty. You must proceed under Rule 26.1.

25.3 EMBEDDED BALL

(A) General Rule. An embedded ball in any closely mown area through the green may be lifted without penalty. A ball is "embedded" when it is in its own pitch-mark and part of the ball is below ground level. A ball doesn't necessarily have to be touching soil to be considered "embedded," since grass and the like may intervene between the ball and the soil.

(B) **Relief Procedures.** Lift the ball, clean it, and drop it as near as possible to the spot where it lay but not nearer the hole. The dropped ball must first strike a part of the course through the green. If the dropped ball rolls into its own pitch-mark, you must re-drop under Rule 20.2(c). If the dropped ball embeds, this Rule 25.3 applies.

25.4 WRONG PUTTING GREEN

(A) **Interference Defined.** Interference from a wrong putting green occurs when a ball is on any putting green other than that of the hole being played, including a practice putting green unless otherwise stated by the Committee. Interference with your stance or the area of your intended swing is not, of itself, interference under this rule.

(B) **Relief Procedures.** If you have interference from a wrong putting green, you must take relief, and there is no penalty. Find the nearest point of relief that is not in a hazard or on a putting green. Lift the ball and drop it within one club-length of the nearest point of relief. The ball may be cleaned when lifted.

25.5 PENALTY. If you violate this Rule 25, you lose the hole in match play or receive a two-stroke penalty in stroke play.

RULE 26. Water Hazards

26.0 DEFINED TERMS. This rule contains the following defined terms:
- hole (35.22);
- lateral water hazard (35.25);
- lost ball (35.29);
- out of bounds (35.35);
- stroke (35.47); and
- water hazard (35.52).

26.1 BALL IN A WATER HAZARD

(A) Status of Ball. If you cannot find your ball and you know or are almost certain that it is lost in a water hazard, then you may apply this Rule 26.1. Otherwise, your ball is considered lost outside the water hazard and you must proceed under Rule 27.1 (stroke and distance).

(B) Procedures. If your ball is found in or is lost in a water hazard (whether or not the ball lies in water), you have the following options:

(1) play the ball as it lies without penalty; or

(2) add a one-stroke penalty and proceed with one of the following choices:

(a) play a ball from the spot where the original ball was last played (see Rule 20.5);

(b) drop a ball behind the water hazard on an imaginary line extending from the hole through the point where the original ball last crossed the margin of the water hazard (without a limit on how far behind the water hazard the ball may be dropped on this imaginary line); or

(c) if the ball last crossed the margin of a lateral

water hazard, drop a ball outside the water hazard, no closer to the hole within two club-lengths of either the point where the original ball last crossed the margin of the lateral water hazard, or the point on the opposite margin of the lateral water hazard equally distant from the hole.

(c) Cleaning Ball. You may clean the ball, or substitute a ball, when proceeding under Rule 26.1(B).

(D) Ball Moving. See Rule 14.6 for a ball moving in water in a water hazard.

26.2 BALL PLAYED FROM WITHIN A WATER HAZARD

(A) The Ball Stops in the Same or Another Water Hazard

(1) If you have played from within a water hazard and your ball stops in the same or another water hazard after the stroke, you have the following choices:

(a) add a one-stroke penalty and play a ball from the spot at which you made the last stroke outside the water hazard (see Rule 20.5); or

(b) proceed under any option in Rule 26.1(B).

(2) If you choose to proceed under Rule 26.1(B)(2)
(a) (dropping a ball in the water hazard at the spot from where you last played), you may choose not to play the dropped ball. You then have the following choices:

(a) proceed under Rule 26.1(B)(2)(b) and add an *additional* one-stroke penalty;

(b) proceed under Rule 26.1(B)(2)(c), if applicable, and add an *additional* one-stroke penalty; or

(c) play a ball from the spot where you made the last stroke outside the water hazard and add an *additional* one-stroke penalty (see Rule 20.5).

(B) Ball Lost or Unplayable Outside the Water Hazard or Out of Bounds. If you have played from within a water hazard and your ball goes out of bounds, or is lost or declared unplayable outside the water hazard and you decide to proceed under stroke and distance, you must take a one-stroke penalty under Rule 27.1 or 28.1(A). You then have the following choices:

(1) play a ball from the spot in the water hazard from where the original ball was last played (see Rule 20.5); or

(2) add an *additional* one-stroke penalty and play a ball from the spot where the last stroke from outside a water hazard was made (see Rule 20.5); or,

(3) proceed under Rule 26.1(B)(2)(b) or, if applicable, Rule 26.1(B)(2)(c); add an *additional* one-stroke penalty; and use the point where the original ball last crossed the margin of the water hazard as a reference point for a proper drop.

(c) Procedural Reminders

(1) When proceeding under Rule 26.2(B), you need not drop a ball as described by Rule 27.1 or 28.1(B). If you drop a ball, you need not play it. You may then proceed under 26.2(B)(2) or (3) above. If you do so, you receive a total of two penalty strokes: one stroke under Rule 27.1 or 28.1(A), and an *additional* penalty stroke for proceeding under Rule 26.1.

(2) If a ball played from within a water hazard is declared unplayable outside the water hazard, you may also choose to proceed under Rule 28.1(B)(2) or 28.1(B)(3).

(D) Penalty. If you violate this Rule 26, you lose the hole in match play or receive a two-stroke penalty in stroke play.

RULE 27.
Ball Lost or Out of Bounds; Provisional Ball

27.0 DEFINED TERMS. This rule contains the following defined terms:
- abnormal ground condition (35.1);
- ball in play (35.4);
- fellow-competitor (35.12(B), (C));
- hole (35.22);
- immovable obstruction (35.33);
- lost ball (35.29);
- obstruction (35.33);
- opponent (35.34);
- out of bounds (35.35);
- partner (35.37);
- penalty stroke (35.38);
- provisional ball (35.39);
- scorer (35.43);
- stroke (35.47);
- teeing ground (35.50);
- water hazard (35.52); and
- wrong ball (35.53).

27.1 BALL LOST OR OUT OF BOUNDS

(A) General Rule. If your ball is lost or out of bounds, you are penalized with "stroke and distance": you take a one-stroke penalty and you must play a ball from the spot where you played the original ball (see Rule 20.5).

(B) Proceeding Under Stroke and Distance. At any time, you may play a ball as nearly as possible from the spot where your original ball was last played (see Rule 20.5), taking a one-stroke penalty. Except as otherwise provided in the rules, if you make a stroke at a ball from the spot where your original ball was last played, you are considered to have proceeded under "stroke and distance."

(c) Exceptions. If you know or are almost certain that your original ball has been moved by an outside agency (Rule 18.1), is in an obstruction (Rule 24.3), is in an abnormal ground condition (Rule 25.2), or is in a water hazard (Rule 26.1), you may proceed under the applicable rule.

(d) Penalty. If you violate this Rule 27.1, you lose the hole in match play or receive a two-stroke penalty in stroke play.

27.2 PROVISIONAL BALL

(a) Procedures

(1) Conditions for Hitting a Provisional Ball. To save time, you may play a provisional ball if your original ball might be either out of bounds or lost outside a water hazard.

(2) Declaring a Provisional Ball. You must announce to your opponent, your scorer, or a fellow-competitor that you intend to play a provisional ball, and you must play it before you or your partner goes forward to search for the original ball.

(3) Failure to Comply. If you fail to follow these procedures before playing another ball, the second ball is not a provisional ball but becomes the ball in play with a penalty of stroke and distance (Rule 27.1(b)). The original ball is then considered lost and, if found, must not be played.

(4) Additional Provisional Balls. If a provisional ball you've played under this rule might be lost outside a water hazard or out of bounds, you may play another provisional ball. Any additional provisional ball bears the same relationship to the previous provisional ball as the first provisional ball bears to the original.

(5) Order of Play. See Rule 10.3 for the order of play from the teeing ground for a provisional ball.

(B) **When Provisional Ball Becomes the Ball in Play**

(1) General. You may play a provisional ball until you reach the area where the original ball is likely to be found. If you make a stroke with the provisional ball from that place, or from a point nearer the hole than that place, the original ball is considered lost and the provisional ball becomes the ball in play under penalty of stroke and distance (Rule 27.1(A)).

(2) Original Ball Lost or Out of Bounds. Once you determine that the original ball is lost or is out of bounds, the provisional ball becomes the ball in play under penalty of stroke and distance (Rule 27.1(A)).

(3) Original Ball in Water Hazard. If you know or are almost certain that the original ball is lost in a water hazard, you may proceed according to Rule 26.1, but you must abandon the provisional ball.

(4) Exception. If you know or are almost certain that the unfound original ball was moved by an outside agency (Rule 18.1), is in an immovable obstruction (Rule 24.3), or in an abnormal ground condition (Rule 25.2), you may proceed under the applicable rule.

(C) **When Provisional Ball Is Abandoned**

(1) General Rule. If the original ball is neither lost nor out of bounds, you must abandon your provisional ball and continue play with the original ball. If you know or are almost certain that the original ball is in a water hazard, the provisional ball must be abandoned and you may proceed under Rule 26. Strokes taken and penalty strokes received by playing a provisional ball that is abandoned under this rule are disregarded.

(2) Penalty. If you fail to abandon the provisional ball when required, any further strokes made with the provisional ball are strokes with a wrong ball and Rule 15 penalties apply.

RULE 28. Unplayable Ball

28.0 DEFINED TERMS. This rule contains the following defined terms:
- bunker (35.6);
- course (35.13);
- hole (35.22);
- stroke (35.47); and
- water hazard (35.52).

28.1 GENERAL RULE AND OPTIONS

(A) Declaring a Ball Unplayable. You may declare your ball unplayable anywhere on the course except in a water hazard. You are the sole judge of whether your ball is unplayable.

(B) Procedures. If you declare your ball unplayable, you are penalized one stroke and must continue as follows:

(1) play a ball from the spot where you last played the original ball (Rule 20.5);

(2) drop a ball within two club-lengths of the spot where the original ball lay, but not nearer the hole; or

(3) drop a ball on an imaginary line extending from the hole through the point where the original ball lay, without limit on how far behind that point the ball may be dropped.

(c) Cleaning Ball. You may clean your ball or substitute a ball when proceeding under this Rule 28.1(B).

28.2 BUNKER RESTRICTION. If the unplayable ball is in a bunker, you may proceed under any option under Rule 28.1(B), but if you choose option (2) or (3), a ball must be dropped in the bunker.

28.3 PENALTY. If you violate this Rule 28, you lose the hole in match play or receive a two-stroke penalty in stroke play.

RULE 29.
Threesomes and Foursomes

29.0 DEFINED TERMS. This rule contains the following defined terms:
- foursome (35.17(C), 35.18(B));
- hole (35.22);
- partner (35.37);
- penalty stroke (35.38);
- putting green (35.40);
- side (35.44);
- stroke (35.47);
- teeing ground (35.50); and
- threesome (35.17(B)).

29.1 GENERAL FORMAT. In threesome or foursome play, the partners play alternately from the teeing ground and alternately during each hole. Penalty strokes do not affect the order of play.

29.2 INCORRECT ORDER IN MATCH PLAY. If you play when your partner should have played, your side loses the hole.

29.3 INCORRECT ORDER IN STROKE PLAY
- **(A) General Penalty.** If your side makes a stroke or strokes in incorrect order, those strokes are canceled, and your side receives a two-stroke penalty.
- **(B) Required Correction.** The side must correct the error by playing a ball in proper order as nearly as possible from the spot where the side played out of order (see Rule 20.5). If the side makes a stroke from the next teeing ground without first correcting the error — or, in the case of the last hole of the round, leaves the putting green without declaring its intention to correct the error — the side is disqualified.

RULE 30.
Three-Ball, Best-Ball, and Four-Ball Match Play

30.0 DEFINED TERMS. This rule contains the following defined terms:
- ball in play (35.4);
- best-ball (35.17(E));
- caddie (35.7);

- Committee (35.11);
- equipment (35.14);
- flagstick (35.15);
- four-ball (35.17(F), 35.18(C));
- handicap (35.20);
- hazard (35.21);
- hole (35.22);
- move (35.30);
- opponent (35.34);
- partner (35.37);
- rule (35.42);
- side (35.44);
- stroke (35.47);
- three-ball (35.17(D)); and
- wrong ball (35.53).

30.1 GENERAL. The normal rules apply to three-ball, best-ball, and four-ball matches, so far as they don't contradict the following special rules.

30.2 THREE-BALL MATCH PLAY

(A) Ball at Rest Moved or Purposely Touched by an Opponent. If your ball is accidentally moved or purposely touched by an opponent or by an opponent's caddie or equipment (other than during a search), Rule 18.3(B) applies. That opponent receives a one-stroke penalty in the match with you, but not in their match with the other opponent.

(B) Ball Deflected or Stopped by an Opponent

(1) General Rule. If your ball is accidentally deflected or stopped by an opponent or an opponent's caddie or equipment, there is no penalty.

(2) Procedure Options. In your match with that opponent, you may play the ball as it lies, or before either side makes another stroke, you may cancel the stroke and play a ball without penalty as near as possible from the spot where the original ball was last played (see Rule 20.5). In your match with the other opponent, the ball must be played as it lies. If you follow the replay option, you will have two balls in play.

(3) Exceptions. For a ball striking a person attending the flagstick, or anything carried by that person, see Rule 17.3(B). For a ball purposely deflected or stopped by an opponent, see Rule 1.2(A).

30.3 BEST-BALL AND FOUR-BALL MATCH PLAY

- **(A) Representing a Side.** A side may be represented by one partner for all or any part of a match. An absent partner may join a match between holes, but not during play of a hole.
- **(B) Order of Play.** Balls belonging to the same side may be played in the order the side considers best.
- **(C) Wrong Ball.** If you make a stroke with a wrong ball, you are disqualified for that hole. But your partner is not penalized, even if the wrong ball belongs to your partner. If the wrong ball belongs to another player, its owner must place a ball on the spot from which the wrong ball was first played. (For returning the ball, see Rule 20.3.)
- **(D) Side Penalized.** A side is penalized if any partner violates any of the following rules:

  (1) Rule 4 (clubs);

  (2) Rule 6.4 (caddie); or

  (3) Any local rule or condition of competition for which the penalty is an adjustment to the score of the match.
- **(E) Side Disqualified**

  (1) One Partner Violates. A side is disqualified for

the match if any partner is disqualified under any of the following rules:

(a) Rule 1.3 (agreeing to waive rules);

(b) Rule 4 (clubs);

(c) Rule 5.1 or 5.2 (the ball);

(d) Rule 6.2(A) (playing off a higher handicap);

(e) Rule 6.4 (having more than one caddie and failing to correct immediately);

(f) Rule 6.7 (repeated delay and slow play);

(g) Rule 11.1 (teeing your ball);

(h) Rule 14.3 (artificial devices, unusual equipment, and abnormal use of equipment); or

(i) Rule 33.1(B) (Committee disqualification).

(2) All Partners Violate. A side is disqualified for the match if all partners are disqualified under any of the following rules:

(a) Rule 6.3 (starting time and groups); or

(b) Rule 6.8 (discontinuing play).

(3) Exceptions. In all other cases where violating a Rule would disqualify you, you are disqualified for that hole only.

(F) Effect of Other Penalties

(1) When Partner Is Helped or Opponent Is Hurt. If your violating a rule helps your partner's play or adversely affects an opponent's play, both you and your partner receive the applicable penalty.

(2) When Partner Isn't Helped and Opponent Isn't Hurt. If your violating a rule does not help your partner's play or adversely affect an opponent's play, the penalty does not apply to your partner. If the penalty is loss of hole, you're the only one disqualified for that hole.

RULE 31. Four-Ball Stroke Play

31.0 DEFINED TERMS. This rule contains the following defined terms:
- caddie (35.7);
- Committee (35.11);
- competitor (35.12);
- equipment (35.14);
- four-ball (35.18(c));
- handicap (35.20);
- hazard (35.21);
- hole (35.22);
- partner (35.37);
- rule (35.42);
- side (35.44);
- stipulated round (35.46);
- stroke (35.47); and
- wrong ball (35.53).

31.1 GENERAL FORMAT
(A) Form of Play. In four-ball stroke play, two competitors play as partners, each playing his or her own ball. The lower score of the partners is the score for the hole. If one partner fails to complete the play of the hole, there is no penalty.

(B) Rules of Golf Apply. The normal rules apply to four-ball stroke play so far as they don't contradict the following special rules.

31.2 REPRESENTING A SIDE. A side may be represented by either partner for all or any part of a stipulated round. Both partners need not be present. An absent competitor may join a partner between holes, but not during play of a hole.

31.3 SCORING. For each hole, only the gross score of whichever partner's score is to count must be recorded. The gross scores to count must be individually identifiable; otherwise, the side is disqualified. Only one of the partners needs to sign the scorecard. (Wrong score recorded — see Rule 31.7(A)(8).)

31.4 ORDER OF PLAY. Balls belonging to the same side may be played in whatever order the side considers best.

31.5 WRONG BALL

(A) If you make a stroke with a wrong ball, you receive a two-stroke penalty for that hole and must then play the correct ball (see Rule 15.3). Your partner is not penalized even if the wrong ball belongs to that partner.

(B) If the wrong ball belongs to another competitor, its owner must place a ball on the spot from where the wrong ball was first played. (For returning the ball, see Rule 20.3.)

31.6 SIDE PENALIZED. A side is penalized if any partner violates any of the following rules:

(A) Rule 4 (clubs);

(B) Rule 6.4 (caddie); or

(C) Any local rule or condition of competition for which the penalty is a maximum penalty per round.

31.7 DISQUALIFICATION PENALTIES

(A) One Partner Violates. A side is disqualified from the competition if either partner is disqualified under any of the following rules:

  (1) Rule 1.3 (agreeing to ignore rules);

  (2) Rule 3.4 (refusing to comply with a rule);

(3) Rule 4 (clubs);

(4) Rule 5.1 or 5.2 (the ball);

(5) Rule 6.2(B) (playing off a higher handicap or failing to record a handicap);

(6) Rule 6.4 (having more than one caddie and failing to correct immediately);

(7) Rule 6.6(B) (signing and returning card);

(8) Rule 6.6(E) (wrong score for hole, i.e., when the recorded score of the partner whose score is to count is lower than actually taken; if the recorded score of the partner whose score is to count is higher than actually taken, it stands as returned);

(9) Rule 6.7 (undue delay and slow play);

(10) Rule 7.1 (practice before or between rounds);

(11) Rule 10.2(C) (sides agree to play out of turn);

(12) Rule 11.1 (teeing your ball);

(13) Rule 14.3 (artificial devices, unusual equipment, or abnormal use of equipment);

(14) Rule 22.4 (ball assisting play);

(15) Rule 31.3 (scores to count not individually identifiable); or

(16) Rule 33.1(B) (Committee disqualification).

(B) Both Partners Violate. A side is disqualified from the competition if:

(1) both partners violate Rule 6.3 (starting time and groups);

(2) both partners violate Rule 6.8 (discontinuing play); or

(3) each partner, on the same hole, violates a rule for which the penalty is disqualification from the competition or that hole.

(C) For the Hole Only. In all other cases, when violating a rule would require disqualification, you're disqualified only for the hole where the violation occurred.

31.8 EFFECT OF OTHER PENALTIES. If your violating a rule helps your partner's play, both you and your partner receive the applicable penalty. In all other cases, if you receive a penalty for violating a rule, the penalty doesn't apply to your partner.

RULE 32.
Bogey, Par, and Stableford Competitions

32.0 DEFINED TERMS. This rule contains the following defined terms:
- caddie (35.7);
- Committee (35.11);
- competitor (35.12);
- equipment (35.14);
- handicap (35.20);
- hole (35.22);
- honor (35.24);
- rule (35.42);
- scorer (35.43); and
- stroke (35.47).

32.1 DEFINITION AND CONDITIONS. In a bogey, par, or Stableford stroke competition, you are playing against a target score for each hole. The rules for stroke play apply so far as they don't contradict the following special rules. In a handicap bogey, par, and Stableford competition, the competitor with the lowest net score on a hole has the honor at the next tee.

(A) Bogey and Par Competitions

(1) Scoring. The scoring for bogey and par competitions is kept by holes, as in match play. If you make a net score less than the target score, you win that hole. A net score equal to the target score is a half. Any other result for a hole, including no score, is a loss. The winner is the competitor with the most winning holes. The scorer is responsible for marking only the gross score for each hole where your net score is equal to or less than the target score.

(2) Penalty Notes

(a) If you violate Rule 4 (clubs), Rule 6.4 (caddie), or any local rule or condition of competition for which there is a maximum penalty per round, and you receive a penalty less than disqualification, your score is adjusted by deducting a hole or holes under the applicable rule. You must report this violation to the Committee or else you're disqualified.

(b) If you miss your starting time (Rule 6.3(B)) but arrive ready to play within five minutes, or violate Rule 6.7 (undue delay or slow play), then your score is adjusted by deducting one hole from the overall result. For repeat violations of Rule 6.7, see Rule 32.2(A).

(c) If you receive the additional two-stroke penalty in the exception to Rule 6.6(E), that additional penalty is applied by deducting one hole from the overall result. The penalty you failed to include applies to the hole where you violated a rule. But neither penalty applies when your violation of Rule 6.6(E) doesn't affect the result of the hole.

(B) Stableford Competition

(1) The scoring in Stableford competition is

made by awarding points relating to a target score at each hole:

Score for Hole	Points
More than one over target score or no score returned	0
One over target score	1
Target score	2
One under target score	3
Two under target score	4
Three under target score	5
Four under target score	6

The winner is the competitor who scores the most points. The scorer is responsible for recording only the gross score at each hole where your net score earns points.

(2) Penalty Notes

(a) If you violate any rule, local rule, or condition of competition for which there is a maximum penalty per round (such as Rule 4 (clubs) or Rule 6.4 (caddie)), your score is adjusted by deducting two points for each hole where a violation occurred, with a maximum deduction of four points per round for each rule breached. You must report the violation to the Committee or else you're disqualified.

(b) If you miss your starting time (Rule 6.3(B)) but arrive ready to play within five minutes, or violate Rule 6.7 (undue delay or slow play), your score is adjusted by deducting two points from the total for the round. For repeat violations of Rule 6.7, see Rule 32.2(A).

(c) If you receive the additional two-stroke penalty in the exception to Rule 6.6(e), that additional penalty is applied by deducting two points from the total points scored for the round. The penalty you failed to include applies to the hole where you violated a rule. But neither penalty applies when your violation of Rule 6.6(e) doesn't affect the points scored on the hole.

(d) **Alternative Penalty.** In a given Stableford competition, the Committee may modify this penalty as follows:

(1) for the first violation, one point deducted;

(2) for the second violation, two additional points deducted; and,

(3) for any further violation, disqualification.

32.2 DISQUALIFICATION PENALTIES

(A) From the Competition. You're disqualified from the competition for incurring a disqualification penalty under any of the following:

(1) Rule 1.3 (agreeing to ignore rules);

(2) Rule 3.4 (refusing to comply with a rule);

(3) Rule 4 (clubs);

(4) Rule 5.1 or 5.2 (the ball);

(5) Rule 6.2(B) (playing off a higher handicap or failing to record a handicap);

(6) Rule 6.3 (starting time and groups);

(7) Rule 6.4 (having more than one caddie and failing to correct immediately);

(8) Rule 6.6(B) (signing and returning card);

(9) Rule 6.6(E) (wrong score for hole; except that there is no penalty when violating this rule doesn't affect the result of the hole);

(10) Rule 6.7 (undue delay and slow play);

(11) Rule 6.8 (discontinuing play);

(12) Rule 7.1 (practice before or between rounds);

(13) Rule 10.2(c) (playing out of turn);

(14) Rule 11.1 (teeing your ball);
(15) Rule 14.4 (artificial devices, unusual equipment, and abnormal use of equipment);
(16) Rule 22.4 (ball assisting play); or
(17) Rule 33.1(B) (Committee disqualification).

(B) For a Hole. In all other cases when violating a rule would require disqualification, you're disqualified only for the hole where the breach occurred.

RULE 33. The Committee

33.0 DEFINED TERMS. This rule contains the following defined terms:
- Committee (35.11);
- competitor (35.12);
- course (35.13);
- four-ball (35.17(F), 35.18(C));
- ground under repair (35.19);
- handicap (35.20);
- hazard (35.21);
- hole (35.22);
- integral part of the course (35.33(A)(3));
- local rule (35.42(C));
- obstructions (35.33);
- out of bounds (35.35);
- putting green (35.40);
- referee (35.41);
- rule (35.42);
- stipulated round (35.46);
- stroke (35.47);
- teeing ground (35.50); and
- water hazard (35.52).

33.1 AUTHORITY AND RESTRICTIONS

(A) General Information. The Committee must state the conditions for a competition. The Committee cannot waive a rule of golf. In stroke play, the Committee may limit a referee's duties. Once a stipulated round has started, the Committee cannot reduce the number of holes for that stipulated round.

(B) Disqualification Penalty. In exceptional cases, a disqualification penalty may be waived, modified, or imposed at the Committee's discretion. Any penalty less than disqualification cannot be waived or modified. The Committee may disqualify you for a serious breach of etiquette (see Appendix 2).

(C) Local Rules

(1) The Committee may provide local rules for abnormal conditions if they are consistent with the policies in Appendix 1 of the Official Rules of Golf published by the USGA.

(2) A local rule cannot waive a rule of golf. Any local rule that purports to do this is void. But if the Committee considers that local abnormal conditions interfere with proper play, the USGA may authorize a local rule modifying the Rules of Golf.

33.2 COURSE RESPONSIBILITIES

(A) Defining the Course. The Committee must accurately define:

(1) the course and out of bounds;

(2) the margins of all water hazards;

(3) ground under repair; and

(4) obstructions and integral parts of the course.

(B) New Holes on the Putting Greens

(1) **Setting of Holes.** Holes should be newly set on the day a stroke competition begins and at other

times as the Committee considers necessary. But all competitors in a single round must play with each hole in the same position.

(2) Exceptions

(a) When it is impossible for a damaged hole to be repaired properly, the Committee may make a new hole during the stipulated round in a nearby similar position.

(b) When a single round is to be played on more than one day, the Committee may provide in the conditions of competition that the holes and teeing grounds may be situated differently on each day of the competition, as long as during any one day of competition, all competitors must play each hole and teeing ground in the same position.

(c) Practice Area. If no practice area is available outside a competition course, the Committee may designate the area where players may practice on the course on any day of a competition. But on any day of a stroke competition, the Committee should not permit practice on or to a putting green or from a hazard on the competition course.

(D) Course Unplayable. If the Committee considers the course not to be in a playable condition or that other circumstances render the proper playing of the game impossible, the Committee may suspend play in match or stroke play or, in stroke play only, cancel play and all scores for the round in question. When a round is canceled, all penalties received during that round are also canceled, including disqualification.

33.3 STARTING TIMES AND GROUPS

(A) The Committee sets the starting times and arranges the groups in which competitors play.

(B) When a match-play competition is played over an extended period, the Committee sets the time limit for each round to be completed. When players are allowed to arrange the date of their match within these limits, the Committee should announce that the match must be played at a stated time on the last day of the period unless the players agree to an earlier date.

33.4 HANDICAP STROKE TABLE. The Committee must publish the order of holes where handicap strokes are given or received.

33.5 DECISION FOR TIES. The Committee must provide for how the winner for a halved match or a tie will be decided. A halved match cannot be decided by stroke play. A tie in stroke play cannot be decided by a match.

33.6 SCORECARD RESPONSIBILITIES
(A) Stroke Play

(1) The Committee must provide an individual scorecard containing the date and the competitor's name or, in foursome or four-ball stroke play, the competitors' names. The committee may request that you record the date and your name on your scorecard.

(2) The Committee is responsible for adding scores and applying the handicap recorded on the scorecard.

(B) Other Competitions

(1) In four-ball stroke play, the Committee is responsible for recording the better-ball score for each hole, applying the handicaps recorded on the scorecard, and adding the better-ball scores.

(2) In bogey, par, and Stableford competitions, the Committee is responsible for applying the handi-

cap recorded on the scorecard and determining the result of each hole and the overall result or points total.

(c) **No Combining Match and Stroke Play.** Certain rules governing stroke play are so different from those governing match play that combining the two forms of play isn't permissible. The results of matches played in these circumstances are not accepted, and in the stroke play competition, the competitors are disqualified.

RULE 34. Disputes and Decisions

34.0 DEFINED TERMS. This rule contains the following defined terms:
- Committee (35.11);
- competitor (35.12);
- handicap (35.20);
- opponent (35.34);
- referee (35.41); and
- rule (35.42).

34.1 TIME LIMITS FOR CLAIMS AND PENALTIES
(A) Match Play
(1) Timely Claims. If a claim is made with the Committee under Rule 2.4, a decision should be given as soon as possible so that the status of the match may be adjusted.

(2) Late Claims

(a) **General Rule.** If a claim is not made within the time limits in Rule 2.4, it will not be considered unless:

(1) it is based on facts previously unknown to the player making the claim; and

(2) the player making the claim had been given wrong information by an opponent (Rules 6.2(b) and 2.5).

(b) **After Results Official, Intent Required.** After the result of the match has been officially announced, no claim can be considered unless the Committee is satisfied that the opponent knowingly gave wrong information. There is no time limit for the Committee to consider this type of claim.

(3) Disqualification Exceptions. There is no time limit on applying the disqualification penalty for breaching Rule 1.3 (agreeing to ignore rules).

(B) **Stroke Play**

(1) When Competition Closed. A competition is considered closed when the result has been officially announced or when the player has teed off in his or her first match after stroke-play qualifying.

(2) No Penalties After Competition Is Closed. No penalty can be rescinded, modified, or imposed after the competition has closed.

(3) Disqualification Exceptions. A disqualification penalty will be imposed after the competition has closed if a competitor:

(a) violated Rule 1.3 (agreeing to ignore rules);

(b) returned a scorecard on which the competitor had provided a handicap knowing that it was higher than allowable and the higher handicap affected the number of strokes received (Rule 6.2(b));

(c) returned a lower score for a hole than actually taken (Rule 6.6(e)) for any reason other than failure to include one or more penalty strokes that the competitor, before the competition closed, didn't know had been incurred; or

(d) knew before the competition closed that he or she had violated any other rule that would have resulted in disqualification.

34.2 REFEREE'S DECISION. A referee who has been appointed by the Committee has the authority to make final decisions (see also Rule 33.1(A)).

34.3 COMMITTEE'S DECISION AND APPEAL

- **(A) Committee as Final Arbiter.** Without an authorized referee, any dispute about the rules should be referred to the Committee, whose decision is final.
- **(B) Referring Inconclusive Point to USGA.** If the Committee can't reach a decision, it should refer the disputed point to the Rules of Golf Committee of the United States Golf Association, whose decision is final.
- **(C) Referral by Players.** If the Committee does not refer a disputed point to the Rules of Golf Committee, the players may prepare an agreed statement through a duly authorized representative of the Committee to the Rules of Golf Committee, requesting an opinion regarding the decision given. The reply will be sent to this authorized representative.
- **(D) Adhering to Rules Required.** The Rules of Golf Committee will not give a decision on any question if play has not been conducted according to the Rules of Golf.

RULE 35. Definitions

35.1 ABNORMAL GROUND CONDITION. An abnormal ground condition on the course is casual water, ground under repair, or any hole, cast, or runway made by a burrowing animal, a reptile, or a bird. A burrowing animal is an animal that makes a hole for habitation or shelter (such as a rabbit, mole, groundhog, gopher, or salamander). A hole made by a nonburrowing animal (such as a dog, squirrel, worm, insect, or the like) is not an abnormal ground condition unless marked as ground under repair (see 35.21).

35.2 ADDRESSING THE BALL. You have addressed the ball when you've grounded your club directly in front of or directly behind your ball, whether or not you've taken your stance.

35.3 ADVICE. Advice is any suggestion that could influence you in determining your play, choice of club, or method of making a stroke. Information on the rules or on matters of public information (such as distances and the position of hazards or the flagstick) is not advice.

35.4 BALL IN PLAY
- **(A) General.** Your ball is in play when you make a stroke on the teeing ground. It remains in play until holed out, except when it is lost, out of bounds, or lifted.
- **(B) Improper Substitution.** If you substitute another ball when the rules do not allow substitution, the substituted ball becomes your ball in play.
- **(C) Marking and Lifting.** If you mark the position of your ball but do not lift it, your ball remains in play.

If you mark, lift, and replace your ball, it is in play whether or not you remove the ball marker.

(D) **Outside the Teeing Ground**

(1) **Starting the Hole.** If you play a ball from outside the teeing ground when starting a hole (or when attempting to correct this mistake), the ball is not in play. Rule 11.4 or 11.5 applies.

(2) **Next-Stroke Exception.** When you elect or are required to make your next stroke from the teeing ground (such as when proceeding under Rule 27 (lost ball)), a ball played from outside the teeing ground is considered to be in play.

(3) **Match-Play Exception.** In match play, if you play a ball outside the teeing ground when starting a hole and your opponent doesn't require you to cancel the stroke according to Rule 11.4(A), your ball is considered to be in play.

35.5 BALL UNFIT FOR PLAY. A ball is unfit for play if it is visibly cut, cracked, or out of shape. A ball is not unfit for play just because mud or other materials stick to it, its surface is scratched, or its paint is damaged.

35.6 BUNKER

(A) **General.** A bunker is a hazard consisting of a prepared area of ground from which turf or soil has been removed and replaced with sand or a similar substance.

(B) **Margins.** The margin of a bunker extends vertically downward, but not upward. Any grass-covered ground bordering or within a bunker, including a stacked-turf face (whether grass-covered or earthen), is not part of the bunker. A wall or lip of the bunker not covered with grass is part of the bunker.

(c) **Status of Ball.** A ball is in a bunker when it lies in or any part of it touches the bunker.

35.7 CADDIE

(A) **General.** A caddie is a person who helps you according to the rules, which may include carrying or handling your clubs during play.

(B) **Multiple Players**

(1) **General.** When you and another player employ one caddie and a rules question arises, the caddie is always considered to be the caddie of the player whose ball (or whose partner's ball) is involved, and equipment carried by the caddie is considered to be that player's equipment.

(2) **Exception.** A caddie acting on specific directions of another player (or the partner of another player) sharing the caddie is considered to be that player's caddie.

35.8 CASUAL WATER

(A) **General.** Casual water is an abnormal ground condition consisting of temporary water on the course (not in a water hazard) that is visible before or after you take your stance.

(B) **Specific Examples**

(1) Snow or natural ice (but not frost) is either casual water or a loose impediment, at your option.

(2) Manufactured ice is an obstruction.

(3) Dew and frost are not casual water.

(C) **Status of Ball.** A ball is in casual water when it touches the casual water.

35.9 CLOSELY MOWN AREA. A closely mown area is any area of the course, including paths through the rough, cut to fairway height or less.

35.10 CLUB UNFIT FOR PLAY. A club is unfit for play if it is substantially damaged — for example, if the shaft is dented, significantly bent, or broken into pieces, or the clubhead becomes loose, detached, or significantly deformed. A club is not unfit for play just because the club's lie or loft has been altered, or the clubhead is scratched.

35.11 COMMITTEE. The Committee is the person or group in charge of the competition or, if the issue does not arise in a competition, in charge of the course.

35.12 COMPETITOR
- **(A)** A competitor is a player in a stroke competition.
- **(B)** A fellow-competitor is any person with whom the competitor plays. Neither is a partner of the other.
- **(C)** In stroke-play foursome and four-ball competitions, where the context so admits, the word *competitor* or *fellow-competitor* includes your partner.

35.13 COURSE. The course is the entire area where play is permitted.

35.14 EQUIPMENT
- **(A) General.** Equipment is anything used, worn, held, or carried by you or your caddie, except:
  - **(1)** any ball you have played at the current hole; or
  - **(2)** any small object (such as a coin or tee) used to mark the position of your ball or the extent of an area for properly dropping a ball under Rule 20.2.
- **(B) Notes.** A ball you have played at the current hole is considered equipment after it is lifted and not put back into play. Rakes and other objects for course care are considered equipment while you or your caddie hold or carry them.

(C) Golf Carts. Equipment includes a golf cart, whether or not motorized. When you, your partner, or either of your caddies moves a shared cart, the cart and all its contents are considered to be your equipment. Otherwise, if a cart is shared by you and another player, the cart and all its contents are considered the equipment of the player whose ball (or whose partner's ball) is involved.

(D) Other Shared Equipment. Other shared equipment is considered to be equipment of the player who last used, wore, held, or carried it. It remains that player's equipment until it is used, worn, held, or carried by another player, that player's partner, or either of their caddies.

35.15 FLAGSTICK. The flagstick is a movable straight indicator, with a circular cross-section, centered in the hole to show its position.

35.16 FORECADDIE. A forecaddie is assigned by the Committee to indicate to players the position of balls during play. A forecaddie is an outside agency (see 35.36).

35.17 FORMS OF MATCH PLAY

(A) Single. A single is a match in which one golfer plays against another.

(B) Threesome. A threesome is a match in which one golfer plays against two, and each side plays one ball.

(C) Foursome. A foursome is a match in which two golfers play against two others, and each side plays one ball.

(D) Three-Ball. A three-ball is a match-play competition in which three golfers play against one another, each playing his or her own ball. Each player is playing in two distinct matches.

(E) Best-Ball. A best-ball is a match in which one golfer plays against the better ball of two or the best ball of three players.

(F) Four-Ball. A four-ball is a match in which two golfers play their best ball against the better ball of two other players.

35.18 FORMS OF STROKE PLAY

(A) Individual. A competition in which each competitor plays as an individual.

(B) Foursome. A competition in which two competitors play as partners and play one ball.

(C) Four-Ball. A competition in which two competitors play as partners, each playing his or her own ball. The lower score of the partners is the score for the hole. If one partner fails to complete a hole, there is no penalty.

(D) Other. For bogey, par, and Stableford competitions, see Rule 32.

35.19 GROUND UNDER REPAIR

(A) General. Ground under repair is any part of the course marked or so declared by the Committee or its representative. It includes material piled for removal and a hole made by a greenkeeper, even if not marked. Ground under repair can be marked after a competition has begun.

(B) Abandoned-Material Exclusion. Grass cuttings and other abandoned materials left on the course and not intended to be removed are not ground under repair unless marked.

(C) Markings and Margins. The margin of ground under repair extends vertically downward, but not upward. Stakes and lines defining ground under repair are considered part of the ground under repair, and these stakes are obstructions (see 35.33). The margin of the ground under repair is defined by the nearest outside points of the stakes at ground level. When both stakes and lines are used, the stakes help identify the ground under repair and the lines define the ground under repair. All ground and any grass, bush, tree, or other growing thing within the ground under repair is part of the ground under repair.

(D) **Status of Ball.** A ball is in ground under repair when it touches the ground under repair or any growing thing considered within the ground under repair.

(E) **Restricting Play.** The Committee may make a local rule prohibiting play from ground under repair or any environmentally sensitive area that has been declared to be ground under repair.

35.20 HANDICAP. A handicap is a numerical measurement of a golfer's skill and potential ability, calculated by comparing recent scores to certain objective standards for each course that you play. By comparing handicaps, players of different skill can compete against each other more fairly. Your handicap for a given competition is determined by comparing your official USGA handicap index with the course handicap table.

35.21 HAZARD. A hazard is any bunker or water hazard.

35.22 HOLE. The hole must be 4¼ inches in diameter and at least 4 inches deep. If a lining is used, it must be sunk at least 1 inch below the putting-green surface, unless the nature of the soil makes this impracticable. The lining's outer diameter must not exceed 4¼ inches.

35.23 HOLE OUT. A ball is holed out when it is at rest within the circumference of the hole and all of the ball is below the level of the hole's lip.

35.24 HONOR. The honor is the entitlement to play first from a teeing ground.

35.25 LATERAL WATER HAZARD

(A) General. A lateral water hazard is a water hazard or that part of a water hazard so positioned that it is not practicable to drop a ball behind the water hazard according to Rule 26.1(B)(2)(b) (compare 35.52(A)).

(B) Markings and Margins. A lateral water hazard must be marked with red stakes and lines. The margin of a lateral water hazard extends vertically upward and downward. All ground or water within the margin of a lateral water hazard is part of the hazard. Stakes and lines defining the margins of a lateral water hazard are in the hazard, and these stakes are obstructions (see 35.33). The margin of the hazard is defined by the nearest outside points of the stakes at ground level. When both stakes and lines are used, the stakes help identify the hazard and the lines define the hazard margin.

(C) Status of Ball. A ball is in a lateral water hazard if it touches any part of the hazard.

(D) Restricting Play

(1) The Committee may make a local rule restricting play from an environmentally sensitive area that has been defined as a lateral water hazard.

(2) The Committee may define a lateral water hazard as a regular water hazard.

35.26 LINE OF PLAY. The line of play is the direction that you intend your ball to take after a stroke, plus a reasonable distance to the left or right of the intended direction. The line of play extends vertically upward from the ground but does not extend beyond the hole.

35.27 LINE OF PUTT. The line of putt is the line that you intend your ball to take after a stroke on the putting green. Except with respect to Rule 16.1(E), the line of putt includes a reasonable distance to the left or right of the intended line but does not extend beyond the hole.

35.28 LOOSE IMPEDIMENT

(A) General. A loose impediment is a natural object such as a stone, leaf, twig, branch, or any piece of dung, as well as a worm, an insect, and the like (plus any casts or heaps made by them). Anything that is fixed, growing, or solidly embedded — or that adheres to the ball — is not a loose impediment.

(B) Specific Examples

(1) Sand and loose soil are loose impediments on the putting green but nowhere else.

(2) Snow or natural ice (but not frost) is either casual water or a loose impediment, at your option.

(3) Manufactured ice is an obstruction.

(4) Dew and frost are not loose impediments.

35.29 LOST BALL. A ball in play is considered lost if:

(A) you haven't found or identified it within five minutes after you, your partner, or your caddies have begun to search for it (time spent playing a wrong ball doesn't count toward the five minutes);

(B) you have made any stroke with a provisional ball from the place where your original ball is likely to be or from a point nearer the hole than that place (the provisional ball then becomes the ball in play (see Rule 27.2(b)));

(c) you have put another ball into play under penalty of stroke and distance (see Rule 26.1(b), Rule 27.1(a), and Rule 28.1(b));

(D) you have put another ball into play because you know or are almost certain that your original ball, which has not been found, has been moved by an outside agency (see Rule 18.1) or is in an obstruction (see Rule 24.3), an abnormal ground condition (see Rule 25.2), or a water hazard (see Rule 26.1); or

(E) you have made a stroke at a substituted ball, even though you may not have searched for your original ball.

35.30 MOVE. A ball moves if it leaves its position and comes to rest in a different position.

35.31 NEAREST POINT OF RELIEF

(A) **General.** The nearest point of relief is the reference point for taking relief without penalty from interference by an immovable obstruction (Rule 24.2), an abnormal ground condition (Rule 25.1), or a wrong putting green (Rule 25.4). It is the point on the course nearest the place where your ball lies, not closer to the hole, and at which, if the ball were so positioned, no interference (from the specific relief situation) would exist.

(B) **Procedures.** You should determine your nearest point of relief by using the club with which you would have made your next stroke to simulate your address position, direction of play, and swing for the stroke as if the condition were not there.

35.32 OBSERVER

(A) Duties. An observer is someone assigned by the Committee to help a referee decide questions of fact and to report any rules violations.

(B) Restrictions. An observer should not attend the flagstick, mark the position of the hole, lift a ball in play, or mark its position.

35.33 OBSTRUCTION

(A) General. An obstruction is anything artificial (including the artificial surfaces and sides of roads and paths, and manufactured ice) but does not include:

(1) an object defining out of bounds (such as a wall, fence, stake, or railing);

(2) any part of an immovable artificial object that is out of bounds; and

(3) any construction that the Committee has declared to be an integral part of the course.

(B) Movable Obstruction. An obstruction is considered movable if it can be moved without unreasonable effort, without unduly delaying play, and without causing damage. Otherwise, it is an immovable obstruction.

(C) Restrictions. By local rule, the Committee may declare a movable obstruction to be an immovable obstruction.

35.34 OPPONENT.
An opponent is a player on a side that your side is competing against in match play.

35.35 OUT OF BOUNDS

(A) General. Out of bounds means beyond the boundaries of the course or any part of the course so declared by the Committee (compare 35.13).

(B) **Markings and Margins.** The out-of-bounds line extends vertically upward and downward. Out-of-bounds indicators should be white. When out of bounds is defined by a line on the ground, the line itself is out-of-bounds. When out of bounds is defined by reference to stakes or a fence, the out-of-bounds line is determined by the nearest inside points of the stakes or fence posts at ground level (excluding angled supports). When both stakes and lines are used to indicate out of bounds, the stakes help identify the out of bounds and the lines define out of bounds. An object defining out of bounds (such as a wall, fence, stake, or railing) is not an obstruction and is considered fixed. But when a line defines out of bounds, stakes that help identify out of bounds may be declared obstructions by the Committee.

(c) **Status of Ball.** A ball is in bounds if any part of it lies in bounds. You may stand out of bounds to play a ball that is in bounds.

35.36 OUTSIDE AGENCY. An outside agency is any person or thing not a part of your match or, in stroke play, not part of your side. The term outside agency includes any ball not played by you or your partner, a referee, a scorer, an observer, an animal, a spectator, a fellow-competitor, and a forecaddie, but not wind or water.

35.37 PARTNER

(A) **Generally.** A partner is a player on your side (see 35.44).

(B) **Other Forms of Play.** In a threesome, foursome, best-ball, or four-ball play, where the context allows, the word *player* includes each of your partners.

35.38 PENALTY STROKE. A penalty stroke is one added to your score or your side's score for violating a rule. In a threesome or foursome, a penalty stroke doesn't affect the playing order.

35.39 PROVISIONAL BALL. A provisional ball is a ball played under Rule 27.2 when your ball may be lost outside a water hazard or may be out of bounds.

35.40 PUTTING GREEN
- **(A) General.** The putting green is all ground that is specially prepared for putting on a given hole, or any other ground as declared by the Committee.
- **(B) Status of Ball.** A ball is on the putting green when any part of it touches the putting green.

35.41 REFEREE
- **(A) Duties.** A referee is appointed by the Committee to decide questions of fact and apply the rules. A referee must act on any rule violation that is reported or that he or she observes.
- **(B) Match Play.** If a referee is assigned to accompany a specific match, the referee must act on any rule violation that he or she observes. Otherwise, in match play a referee may only intervene in matters concerning Rule 1.3, Rule 6.7, or Rule 33.1(B).
- **(C) Restrictions.** A referee should not attend the flagstick, mark the position of the hole, lift a ball, or mark its position.

35.42 RULE. The term *rule* includes:
- **(A)** any Rule of Golf and its interpretation as contained in the Decisions on the Rules of Golf;
- **(B)** any condition of competition made by the Committee under Rule 33.1(A);

(c) any local rule made by the Committee under Rule 33.1(c); and

(d) any specification on equipment in Appendixes 2, 3, and 4 in the USGA Official Rules of Golf and interpretations contained in "A Guide to the Rules on Clubs and Balls."

35.43 SCORER. A scorer is one appointed by the Committee to record a competitor's score in stroke play. A scorer may be a fellow-competitor but not a referee.

35.44 SIDE. A side is a player or two or more players who are partners. In match play, each player on the opposing side is an opponent. In stroke play, all players are competitors and different sides playing together are fellow-competitors.

35.45 STANCE. You have taken your stance when you have placed your feet in position to prepare for making a stroke.

35.46 STIPULATED ROUND. The stipulated round consists of 18 holes of the course played in their correct order, unless the Committee authorizes a different order or fewer holes. See Rule 2.1(B) for extending the stipulated round in match play.

35.47 STROKE. A stroke is the forward movement of the club made with the intention of striking at and moving your ball. If you voluntarily stop your downswing before your clubhead reaches the ball, you have not taken a stroke.

35.48 SUBSTITUTED BALL. A substituted ball is a ball you've put into play for your original ball when it was in play, lost, out of bounds, or lifted, whether or not the substitution was permitted. A substituted ball becomes the ball in play when you've dropped or placed it (see Rule 20.4).

35.49 TEE. A tee is a device designed to raise the ball off the ground. It must not be longer than four inches, and it must not be manufactured in any way that could indicate the line of play or affect the ball's movement.

35.50 TEEING GROUND
- **(A) General.** The teeing ground is the starting place for the hole to be played. It is a rectangular area two club-lengths in depth, the front and sides of which are defined by the outside limits of two tee markers.
- **(B) Status of Ball.** A ball is inside the teeing ground when any part of it touches or lies inside the area's defined margins.

35.51 THROUGH THE GREEN. Through the green means the whole area of the course except:
- **(A)** the teeing ground and putting green of the hole you're playing; and
- **(B)** a hazard anywhere on the course.

35.52 WATER HAZARD
- **(A) General.** A water hazard is any sea, lake, pond, river, ditch, surface drainage ditch, and anything of a similar nature (whether or not containing water).
- **(B) Markings and Margins.** Water hazards (other than lateral water hazards) must be marked by yellow stakes and lines. The margin of a water hazard extends vertically upward and downward. All ground or water within the margin of a water hazard is part of the hazard. Stakes and lines defining the margins of a water hazard are in the hazard, and

these stakes are obstructions (see 35.33). The margin of the hazard is defined by the nearest outside points of the stakes at ground level. When both stakes and lines are used, the stakes help identify the hazard and the lines define the hazard margin.

(c) Status of Ball. A ball is in a water hazard if it touches any part of the hazard.

(D) Restricting Play. The Committee may by local rule restrict play from an environmentally sensitive area that has been defined as a water hazard.

35.53 WRONG BALL

(A) General. A wrong ball is any ball other than:

(1) your ball in play (including an improperly substituted ball—see 35.4(B) and 35.48). A substituted ball becomes the ball in play when you've dropped or placed it (see Rule 20.4);

(2) a provisional ball (see 35.39) that you've played under Rule 27.2; or

(3) a second ball that you've played under Rule 3.4 or Rule 20.7(c)(2) in stroke play.

(B) Examples. If you make a stroke at another player's ball, an abandoned ball, or your original ball when it's no longer in play, you've played a wrong ball, and Rule 15.2 or 15.3 applies.

35.54 WRONG PUTTING GREEN.
A wrong putting green is any putting green other than the one on the hole you're playing. A practice putting green or pitching green on the course is also a wrong putting green, unless the Committee declares otherwise.

APPENDIX 1. Penalty Summary Chart

1. General Penalty. If you violate a rule, you lose the hole in match play or receive a two-stroke penalty in stroke play.

2. One-Stroke Penalty: Match Play or Stroke Play. If you violate the following rules, you receive a one-stroke penalty:

Rule 5.3 (ball unfit for play —
   procedure violation);
Rule 6.8(c) (lifting ball when play stopped);
Rule 12.2 (identifying ball —
   procedure violation);
Rule 14.4 (striking ball more than once);
Rule 16.2 (ball overhanging hole —
   time violation);
Rule 18.2 (ball at rest moved by you —
   general);
Rule 19.2 (ball moving after stroke deflected by
   you);
Rule 20.1 (lifting or marking position —
   procedure violation);
Rule 20.2 (dropping your ball —
   procedure violation);
Rule 20.3 (placing your ball — procedure violation);
Rule 21 (cleaning ball when not allowed);
Rule 23.2 (ball at rest moved by you —
   after moving a loose impediment);
Rule 24 (obstruction —
   dropping out of a bunker);

Rule 25 (abnormal ground condition—
dropping out of a bunker);
Rule 26 (water-hazard relief);
Rule 27 (ball lost or out of bounds); or
Rule 28 (ball unplayable).

3. One-Stroke Penalty: Match Play Only. If Rule 18.3(B) (ball at rest moved by opponent, not during a search) is violated, the opponent, not the player, receives a one-stroke penalty.

4. Correct or Disqualification. If you violate the following rules and don't correct your mistake, you're disqualified:

Rule 3.3 (failing to hole out in stroke play);
Rule 11.4 (playing from outside teeing ground in stroke play);
Rule 11.5 (playing from wrong teeing ground in stroke play);
Rule 15.3 (playing a wrong ball in stroke play);
Rule 20.7 (playing from a wrong place in stroke play—serious breach); or
Rule 29.3 (threesomes or foursomes—playing in wrong order).

5. Helpful Principles

(A) Whenever you are taking free relief without a penalty (Rules 23, 24, and 25) you must continue play with the same ball. If you don't, you will be penalized for an improper substitution (Rule 15.1(B)). Whenever you are taking relief with a penalty (Rules 26 and 28), you may substitute a ball.

(B) Whenever you drop out of a hazard, you will receive a penalty stroke.

(c) Under the rules, when your ball is *on* or touching the border of a certain area of the course (such as a teeing ground, putting green, hazard, or abnormal ground condition), your ball is considered *in* that area.

APPENDIX 2. Golf Etiquette

1. BE COURTEOUS ON THE COURSE.

(A) The Spirit of the Game. Golf is almost always played without a referee or umpire, so it's up to the players to make the game fair and enjoyable for everyone. Be courteous and show consideration for other players. Play by the rules, no matter how high or low the stakes are. This is the spirit of golf.

(B) Safety. Before playing a stroke or making a practice swing, make sure that no one is standing nearby. You shouldn't risk hitting someone with the club. But more than that, you shouldn't kick up any stones, pebbles, twigs, or turf that might hit someone. If you see golf-course employees nearby or ahead of you, warn them before the stroke. And if you hit the ball and then realize that it might strike someone, immediately shout "Fore!"

(C) Consideration. Three points. First, whoever has the honor should be allowed to play before anyone else. On the teeing ground, don't tee your ball before it's your turn to play. Second, never move, talk, make unnecessary noise, or stand close to or directly behind someone who's addressing the ball or making a stroke. If you have an electronic device of any kind with you, turn it off or set it to alert you silently. And on the putting green, never cast a shadow on or stand in another player's line of putt. Third, never play until the players in front of you are out of range.

(D) Scoring. In stroke play, if you're the one keeping score, make sure you record each player's score correctly before you get to the next tee.

(E) Pace of Play. Play without delay. It's in everyone's interest. If you believe your ball may be lost outside a water hazard or out of bounds, play a provisional ball to save time. (For the correct procedure, see Rule 27.2.) If you're searching for a ball, signal the players behind you to pass as soon as it becomes apparent that the ball won't easily be found. Don't search for five minutes before doing this. And then, when a group is playing through, wait until those players are out of range before continuing to play. When you've finished playing a hole, leave the putting green immediately. If your group ever fails to keep its place on the course and loses more than one clear hole on the players in front, invite the group following you to play through. The Committee may establish pace-of-play guidelines for players to follow.

2. UNDERSTAND PRIORITY ON THE COURSE. In the absence of special rules, a group's pace of play determines priority. A group playing a whole round gets to play through a group playing a shorter round.

3. TAKE CARE OF THE COURSE.

(A) Holes in Bunkers. Before leaving a bunker, carefully fill up and smooth over all holes and footprints — even the ones you didn't make. If a rake is available, use it.

(B) Divots, Ball-Marks, and Spike Marks. Carefully repair all divots and ball-marks that you make. On the greens, quickly repair any noticeable ball-marks that other groups have made. Once you complete a hole, quickly repair any spike marks left on the green.

(C) Avoiding Damage with a Club. When you take a

practice swing — particularly on the tee — avoid making a divot (which damages the course unnecessarily). Never pound the clubhead into the ground.

(D) Damage to Greens. When putting down a bag, be careful not to damage the green or the fringe. When handling the flagstick, don't damage the hole — as you might through careless mishandling of the flagstick or by standing too close to the hole. When standing on the green, don't lean on your putter, particularly when you're removing the ball from the hole. Once you've finished the hole, put the flagstick back carefully, in a perfectly upright position.

(E) Golf Carts. Strictly follow all local notices regulating the movement of golf carts.

4. YOU CAN BE PENALIZED FOR BREACHES OF ETIQUETTE.

(A) Disqualification. Under Rule 33.1(B), the Committee may disqualify a player who commits a serious breach of etiquette.

(B) Ban from Playing. If you continually ignore these etiquette guidelines, you may (among other penalties) be barred from playing on the course for a certain period or from participating in a set number of tournaments.

INDEX

abnormal ground condition
    ball lost in, 25.2, 27.1(B)
    ball moved in search, 12.1(E)
    bunker, 25.1(B)(2)
    burrowing animal hole, 35.1
    casual water, 35.1
    cleaning ball, 25.1(D)(2)
    defined, 35.1
    embedded ball, 25.3
    ground under repair, 35.19, 35.1
    hole from non-burrowing animal, 35.1
    interference, 25.1(A)
    nearest point of relief, 35.31
    putting green, 25.1(B)(3)
    re-drop procedures, 20.2(C)(1)
    relief, 25.1(B)
    searching for ball in, 12.1(E)
    substituting ball, 25.1(D)(1)
    through the green, 25.1(B)(1)
    unreasonable situation, 25.1(C)(2)
    water hazard, 25.1(C)(1)
abnormal use of equipment, 14.4
addressing the ball
    ball moving after address, 18.2
    defined, 35.2
    for determining nearest point of relief, 35.31(B)
    line of putt touched, 16.1(A)(2)
agreeing to ignore rules, 1.3
advice
    defined, 35.3
    giving and asking for, 8.1
    team competitions, 8.3
anchoring defined, 14.2
anchoring the club prohibited, 14.2
anchoring penalty, 14.2
artificial devices, 14.4
artificial objects, See *obstructions*
assistance
    ball assisting another's play, 22.1
    no physical help or assistance when making a stroke, 14.3

ball
- addressing, See *addressing the ball*
- assisting play, 22
- ball lost or out of bounds, 27.1
- ball lost or unplayable outside water hazard or out of bounds (after playing from a water hazard), 26.2(b)
- broken ball, 5.4
- cleaning, 21
- damaged ball, 5.3
- deflected or stopped, 19
- dropping and re-dropping, 20.2
- embedded, 25.3
- exchanged balls (match play), 15.2(c)
- exerting influence on, 1.2(a)
- falling off tee on teeing ground, 11.3, 14.5(b)(i)
- foreign-material restriction, 5.2
- generally, 5.1
- hole out, 35.23
- identifying, 12.2
- in casual water, 35.8(c)
- incorrectly substituted, dropped, or placed, 20.6
- influencing movement of, 1.2(a)
- in ground under repair, 35.19(d)
- in hazard, playing as it lies, 13.4, 26.1(b)(i), 26.2
- in lateral water hazard, 35.25(c)
- in motion, 14.6, 19
- in play, defined, 35.4
- in play, out of play, 20.4(a)
- interfering with or assisting play, 22
- in water hazard, 26, 35.52(c)
- lie, 13.2, 20.3(c)
- lifting, 20.1
- lost ball, defined, 35.29
- lost in abnormal ground condition, 25.2
- lost in obstruction, 24.3
- marking and lifting, 20.1
- movement of ball at rest, 18
- move or moved, defined, 35.30
- moving ball, deflected or stopped, 19
- moving ball, playing, 14.6
- obstruction and, 24.1
- overhanging hole, 16.2
- placing or returning, 20.3
- playing ball as it lies, 13

playing from outside the teeing ground, 11.4, 35.4
playing from a water hazard, 26.2
playing from wrong place (match play), 20.7(B)
playing from wrong place (stroke play), 20.7(C)
playing while moving, 14.6
provisional ball, 27.2
resting against flagstick, 17.4
searching for, 12.1, 13.4(B)(1)
seeing while making stroke, 12.1
specifications, conforming to, 5.1
striking, 14
striking flagstick or attendant, 17.3
substituted, See *substituted ball*
teeing, 11.1
touched by opponent, 18.3
touched by player, 18.2
touching casual water, 35.8(C)
touching ground under repair, 35.19(D)
touching lateral water hazard, 35.25(C)
touching water hazard, 26, 35.52(C)
unfit for play, 5.3, 35.5
unplayable ball, 28
wrong ball, See *wrong ball*

ball marker
moved while removing loose impediment, 23.2
moved while repairing putting green, 16.1(C)
moved while re-placing ball, 20.3(A)(2)
using generally, 20.1(B)(2)
whether ball is in play, 35.4(C), 20.4(A)

ball marks
repairing, 16.1(C)

ball moved
after address, 18.2
after loose impediment is touched, 23.2
by another ball, 18.5
by fellow-competitor, caddie, or equipment (stroke play), 18.4
by opponent, caddie, or equipment (match play), 18.3
by outside agency, 18.1
by player, partner, caddie, or equipment, 18.2
defined, 35.30
during search, 18.2(C)(2)
generally, 1.2, 18
in measuring distance from hole, 18.6
in removing ball-marker, 20.1(C)(1)

ball moved (*continued*)
    in re-creating lie after search, 12.1(A), 18.2(C)(2)
    in removing loose impediment, 23.2
    in removing movable obstruction, 24.1(A)(2)
    in searching for ball covered by sand, 12.1(B)
    in searching for ball in abnormal ground condition or obstruction, 12.1(E)
    in searching for ball in covered hazard, 12.1(C)
    in searching for ball in water hazard, 12.1(D)
    penalty if ball moves after address, 18.2(B)
    playing moving ball, 14.6

ball moving
    after address, 18.2
    deflection on purpose by player, partner, or caddie, 1.2(D), 14.6(C)(2), 19.1(C)
    falling off tee, 11.3, 14.6(B)(1)
    general prohibition on playing, 14.6(A)
    in water hazard, playing, 14.6(B)(3), 14.7
    moving after stroke begins, 14.6(C)
    multiple strikes, 14.6(B)(2)

best-ball match play
    absent partner, 30.3(A)
    defined, 35.17(E)
    disqualification, 30.3(E)
    14-club maximum, 30.3(D)
    order of play, 30.3(B)
    penalties other than disqualification, 30.3(F)
    representing a side, 30.3(A)
    Rules of Golf apply, 30.1
    side disqualified, 30.3(E)
    transferring penalty to partner, 30.3(F)
    wrong ball, 30.3(C)

bogey, par, and Stableford competitions
    bogey and par competitions, 32.1(A)
    disqualification from the competition, 32.2(A)
    disqualification from a hole, 32.2(B)
    generally, 32
    returning a scorecard without including an unknown penalty, 32.1(A)(2)(C), 32.1(B)(2)(C)
    Stableford competition, 32.1(B)

building a stance, 13.3

bunker
    abnormal ground condition, 25.1(B)(2)
    ball in immovable obstruction, 24.3(C)(2)

ball lost in abnormal ground condition, 25.2(B)(2)
defined, 35.6
margins, 35.6(B)
nearest point of relief, 24.2(B)(2), 25.1(B)(2)
relief from immovable obstruction, 24.2(B)(2)
turf face, 35.6(B)
unplayable ball in, 28.2
burrowing animal, defined, 35.1
caddie
    attending flagstick, 17
    ball moved by, 18.2, 18.3, 18.4
    Committee restrictions, 6.4(C)
    defined, 35.7
    multiple players, 35.7(B)
    one-caddie restriction, 6.4(D)
    permitted actions, 6.4(A)
    position of, 8.2(A)(2), 8.2(B)(2), 8.2(C)
    rule violations by, 6.4(B)
casual water
    ball touching, 35.8(C)
    defined, 35.8
    examples of, 35.8(B)
chipping
    practice before round, 7.1(B)(2)
    practice during round, 7.2(B)
claims in match play
    continuing play after claim when Committee unavailable, 2.4(B)(3)
    invoking the rules, 2.4(A)
    late claims, 2.4(B)(4)
    procedures and decisions, 2.4(B)
    second ball in match play, 2.4(B)(3)
    time limits, 34.1(A)
cleaning the ball
    abnormal ground condition, 25.1(D)(2)
    after lifting generally, 21
    ball in water hazard, 26.1(C)
    not allowed when lifting ball that affects play, 22.3
    relief from immovable obstruction, 24.2(B)(4)
    relief from movable obstruction, 24.1(C)(2)
    unplayable ball generally, 28.1(C)
closely mown area
    defined, 35.9
    embedded ball in, 25.3

clubhead
- loose or detached, 35.10
- only part of club for striking ball, 14.1
- stopping clubhead before completing stroke, 35.47

clubs
- adding clubs, 4.3(A)
- carrying a nonconforming club, 4.1(E)
- changing playing characteristics, 4.1(B)
- conforming to usga specifications, 4.1(A)
- damaged clubs, 4.2
- declared out of play, 4.3(D)
- extra club declared out of play, 4.3(D)
- foreign materials on, 4.1(C)
- generally, 4
- grip, artificial aid with, 14.3(B)(1)
- grounding in a hazard, 13.4(A)(2)
- grounding lightly, 13.2(A)(2)
- improper club carried but not used, 4.1(E)(2)
- maximum number of, 4.3
- original design and changes, 4.1
- placing in hazard, 13.4(B)(2)
- replacement during round, 4.2(B)(1)(C)
- selecting clubs for play, 4.3(A)
- sharing clubs, 4.3(B)
- touching ground or water in hazard, 13.4(A)(2), 13.4(B)(2)(b), 13.4(B)(5)
- unfit for play, defined, 35.10
- wear and alteration, 4.1(D)

club unfit for play,
- defined, 35.10
- replacing, 4.2(B)(1)(C)

Committee
- adding scores and applying handicaps, 6.6(F), 33.6
- alternative penalty for tardiness, 6.3(B)
- authority and restrictions, 33.1
- conditions for competition, 33.1(A)
- continuing play after claim when Committee unavailable, 2.4(B)(3)
- course responsibilities, 33.2
- decisions, finality of, 34.3(A)
- decisions for ties, 33.5
- declaring course unplayable, 33.2(D)
- declaring movable obstruction to be immovable, 35.33(C)
- declaring obstruction an integral part of course, 33.2(A)(4)

    defined, 35.11
    defining lateral water hazard as regular water hazard, 35.25(D)(2)
    defining margins of course, 33.2(A)
    defining practice area, 33.2(C)
    denying relief from abnormal ground condition that affects stance only, 25.1(A)(2)
    discretion with disqualification penalty, 33.1(B)
    duties and powers generally, 33
    extending stipulated round for playoff, 2.1(B)
    group assignments, 6.3(C)
    handicap stroke table, 33.4
    limiting a referee's duties, 33.1(A)
    local rules, 33.1(C)
    new holes on the putting greens, 33.2(B)
    practice area, 33.2(C)
    practice regulations, 7.2(C)(1), 7.3
    preventing slow play, 6.7(A)
    promptness of decisions, 2.4(B)(2)
    reducing the number of holes in a stipulated round, 33.1(A)
    restricting caddies, 6.4(C)
    restricting play from ground under repair, 35.19(E)
    restricting play from lateral water hazard, 35.25(D)(1)
    restricting play from water hazard, 35.52(D)
    restricting practice during round, 7.2(C)
    restricting relief from obstructions, 24.2(D)(2)
    resumption of play after suspension, 6.8(D)
    scorecard responsibilities, 33.6
    setting holes, 33.2(B)(1)
    starting time and ending time, 6.3(A), 33.3(A)
    suspending play, 6.8(B)
competitor
    ball in motion striking, 19.4
    defined, 35.12
    failing to hole out, 3.3
    fellow-competitor, 35.12(B), (C)
    playing out of turn, 10.2(C)
    playing outside teeing ground, 11.4(B)
    playing with wrong ball, 15.3
    refusing to comply with a rule, 3.2(B)
    scoring responsibilities, 6.6
concession (match play)
    conceding a stroke, hole, or match, 2.3
    practice after, 7.2(C)(2)

conditions of competition
    Committee to establish, 33.1(A)
    player's responsibility for knowing, 6.1
course
    Committee defining, 33.2(A)
    defined, 35.13
    defining margins of, 33.2(A)(1)
    dropped ball striking, 20.2(A)(2)
    practice on, 7
    unplayable, 33.2(D)
damaged ball
    procedures, 5.3(A)
    unfit for play, 5.3
damaged clubs
    club unfit for play, 35.10
    damaged before round, 4.2(A)
    damaged in normal course of play, 4.2(B)
    damaged in other than normal course of play, 4.2(C)
    generally, 4.2
decisions
    Committee decisions, 2.4(B), 34.3
    fairness in, 1.4
    referee decisions, 34.2
deflecting ball, 19
    intentionally deflecting ball, 1.2(A)
    procedures for ball intentionally deflected, 19.1(C)
delay
    ball overhanging hole, 16.2
    pace of play, 6.7
    undue delay between holes, 6.7(C)
discontinuing play, 6.8
disputes and decisions (match play)
    disqualification, 34.1(A)(3)
    generally, 2.4
    issues not covered by rules, 1.4
    late claims, 34.1(A)(2)
    timely claims, 34.1(A)(1)
disputes and decisions (stroke play)
    adhering to rules required, 34.3(D)
    closing of competition defined, 34.1(B)(1)
    Committee as final arbiter, 34.3(A)
    Committee's decision and appeal, 34.3
    disqualification penalty, 34.1(B)(3)
    issues not covered by rules, 1.4
    no penalties after competition closed, 34.1(B)(2)

INDEX

referee's decision final, 34.2
reference by players, 34.3(C)
disqualification, See *Appendix 1: Penalty Summary Chart*
distance-measuring device, 14.4(A)(2), 14.4(B)(3)
dropping and re-dropping the ball
    ball rolling when dropped, 20.2(C)
    ball striking the course, 20.2(A)(2)
    by whom and how, 20.2(A)
    dropping in a wrong place, 20.7(A)(1)
    embedded ball, 25.3(B)
    from wrong putting green, 25.4(B)
    generally, 20.2
    how to drop, 20.2(A)(1)
    invalid drop, 20.2(A)(3)
    lifting ball incorrectly dropped, 20.6
    near specific spot, 20.2(B)
    placing ball after unsuccessful drops, 20.2(C)(2)
    procedure, 20.2(A)
    touching player or equipment, 20.2(A)(3)
    when ball becomes "in play," 20.4(A)
    when ball in water hazard, 26.1(B)(2)
    when to re-drop, 20.2(C)
    where to drop, 20.2(B)
embedded ball, 25.3(A)
environmentally sensitive area
    declared ground under repair, 35.19(E)
    declared lateral water hazard, 35.25(D)
    restricted play in water hazard, 35.52(D)
equipment
    abnormal use of, 14.4
    artificial device, allowed use of, 14.4(B)(2)
    ball deflected by fellow-competitor, 19.4
    ball deflected by opponent's, 19.3
    ball deflected by your, 19.2
    ball moved by fellow-competitor's (stroke play), 18.4
    ball moved by opponent's (match play), 18.3
    ball moved by your, 18.2
    carts, 35.14(C)
    defined, 35.14
    medical equipment or devices, 14.4
    shared equipment, 35.14(D)
    unusual equipment and artificial devices, 14.4
    Etiquette, Golf, Appendix 2
fairness in deciding disputes, 1.4
falling of player, 13.4(B)(2)(b)

fellow-competitor
- ball moved by, 18.4
- defined, 35.12(B)
- disputing claim of unfit ball, 5.3(A)
- examining ball, 5.3(A)(2)
- identifying ball, 12.2
- struck by ball in motion, 19.1(C), 19.4

flagstick
- attended, held up, or removed, 17.1
- authorized attendance, 17.1(B)
- ball resting against, 17.4
- ball striking flagstick or attendant, 17.3
- defined, 35.15
- moving attended flagstick while ball is in motion, 24.1(B)
- unauthorized attendance, penalty, 17.2
- what is allowed, 17.1(A)

forecaddie, 35.16
foreign materials on clubs, 4.1(C)

four-ball match play
- absent partner, 30.3(A)
- defined, 35.17(F)
- 14-club maximum, 30.3(D)
- order of play, 30.3(B)
- representing a side, 30.3(A)
- Rules of Golf apply, 30.1
- side disqualified, 30.3(E)
- side disqualified exceptions, 30.3(E)(3)
- transference of penalty to partner, 30.3(F)
- wrong ball, 30.3(C)

four-ball stroke play
- absent partner, 31.2
- defined, 35.18
- disqualification penalties, 31.7
- effect of non-disqualification penalties, 31.8
- format, 31.1
- 14-club maximum, 31.6
- general form of play, 31.1(A)
- playing order, 31.4
- representing a side, 31.2
- Rules of Golf apply, 31.1(B)
- scoring, 31.3
- wrong ball, 31.5

foursomes
- defined, 35.17(C), 35.18(B)

general format, 29.1
incorrect order (match play), 29.2
incorrect order (stroke play), 29.3
game of golf
agreement to ignore rules, 1.3
defined, 1.1
description, 1.1
issues not covered by rules, 1.4
primary rules, 1.2
golf carts, 35.14(C)
grass
bordering bunker, 35.6(B)
cuttings not ground under repair, 35.19(B)
touching in finding or identifying ball, 12.1(A)
touching with club in hazard, 13.4
green, See *putting green*
greenkeeper
materials and holes left by, 35.19(A)
ground under repair
abandoned-material exclusion, 35.19(B)
ball lost in abnormal ground condition, 25.2
ball moved in search, 12.1
ball touching, 35.19(D)
defined, 35.19(A)
designated by Committee, 33.2(A)(3)
markings and margins, 35.19(C)
relief, 25.1(B)
water hazard exception, 25.1(C)
handicap
applying to score (Committee responsibility), 33.6(A)(2)
defined, 35.20
handicap stroke table, 33.4
knowingly playing off inflated handicap (stroke play), 34.1(B)(3)(b)
match play, 6.2(A)
player's responsibilities, 6.2
stroke play, 6.2(B)
hazard
ball in, 13.4
bunker as, 35.6(A)
defined, 35.21
dropped ball rolling into, 20.2(C)(1)
grounding club in, 13.4(A)
loose impediments covering ball in, 12.1(C)
loose impediments in, generally, 23.1

hazard (*continued*)
- placing clubs in, 13.4(B)(2)
- practice prohibited in, 7.2(B)
- previous stroke played from, 20.5(A)(2)
- searching for ball covered in, 12.1(C)
- smoothing sand in, 13.4(B)(4)
- testing condition of hazard, 13.4(A)(1)
- touching a loose impediment, 13.4(A)(3)
- touching an obstruction, 13.4(B)(6)
- touching the ground or water, 13.4(A)(2), 13.4(B)(2)(b)
- touching ground in hazard after stroke, 13.4(B)(4) and (5)
- water hazard, See *water hazard*

hole
- ball overhanging, 16.2
- conceding (match play), 2.3
- damaged, 33.2(B)(2)
- defined, 35.22
- halved, 2.1(A)
- number of holes in stipulated round, 35.46
- setting holes (Committee), 33.2(B)(1)
- winning (match play), 2.1(A)
- wrong score for, 6.6(E)

holed ball, defined, 35.23

hole plugs, repairing, 16.1(C)

holing out
- ball played from teeing ground, 1.1, 15.1(A)
- failing to hole out, 3.3

honor
- defined, 35.24
- determining, 10.1(A), 10.2(A)

identifying ball
- general rule, 12.2(A)
- penalties incurred in, 12.2(C)
- procedures, 12.2(B)

information about strokes taken (match play)
- asking, 2.5(A)(1)
- disclosing a penalty, 2.5(A)(2)
- not disclosing a penalty, 2.5(A)(3)
- penalty for wrong information, 2.5(B)

informing scorer about penalty (stroke play), 3.1(B)

irregularities of surface
- generally, 13.2(A)(1)(b)
- teeing ground, 11.1

lateral water hazard
- abnormal ground conditions in, 25.1(C)

ball touching, 35.25(c)
defined, 35.25
markings and margins, 35.25(b)
obstructions in, 24.2(c)
relief options, 26.1(b)(2)(c)
leaving the course, 6.8(a)(4)
lie of ball
    altered, 20.3(c)
    generally, 1.2(b), 13.1
    improving in hazard, 13.4(b)(3)
lifting of ball
    abnormal ground condition, 25.1(b)
    and cleaning, 21.1
    ball incorrectly substituted, dropped, or placed, 20.6
    ball interfering with or assisting play, 22.1
    damaged ball, 5.3(a)(1)
    equipment, 35.14(a)(3)
    for identification, 12.2
    how to mark and lift, 20.1(b)
    improper lifting, 18.2(a)
    in hazard, 12.2, 13.4(b)(2)(b), 14.6(a)
    in or on a movable obstruction, 24.1(a)(3)
    in or on an immovable obstruction, 24.2(b)
    in water hazard, 26.1(c)
    marking and lifting ball generally, 20.1
    on putting green, 16.1(b)
    penalty, See *Appendix 1: Penalty Summary Chart*
    to determine fitness, 5.3(a)(1), (2)
    when another ball is in motion, 16.1(b), 22.2
    when out of play, 35.4(a)
    when play is suspended, 6.8(c)
    who may lift, 20.1(a)
    without good reason, 12.2
lightning as cause for stopping play, 6.8(a)(1)(b)
line of play
    ball anywhere but on putting green, 8.2(a)
    ball on putting green, 8.2(b)
    conforming tee, 35.49
    defined, 35.26
    hindrance in, 24.2(a), 25.1(a)
    improving (restrictions), 11.2, 12.1(a), 13.2
    indicating, 8.2
    indicating in team competitions, 8.3
    in team competition, 8.3
    moving tee marker to improve, 11.2

line of play (*continued*)
- position of caddie, partner, or partner's caddie, 8.2(A)(2), 8.2(C)

line of putt
- defined, 35.27
- hindrance by abnormal ground condition, 25.1(A)
- hindrance by immovable obstruction, 24.2(A)
- pointing out line for putting, 8.2(B)
- position of caddie, partner, or partner's caddie, 8.2(B)(2), 8.2(C)
- removal of loose impediments, 16.1(A)(1)
- repair of hole plugs, ball marks, and other damage, 16.1(C)
- standing astride or on, 16.1(E)
- touching, 16.1(A)

local rules
- as part of a competition, 35.42(C)
- cannot waive a rule of golf, 33.1(C)(2)
- Committee responsibilities, 33.1(C)
- denying relief when only stance is affected by abnormal ground condition, 25.1(A)(2)
- must be consistent with the Official Rules of Golf, 33.1(C)(1)
- nearest point of relief, modified by, 24.2(D)(2)
- restricting play from environmentally sensitive area or ground under repair, 35.19(E), 35.52(D)

loose impediment
- ball moved after touching, 23.2
- covering ball in hazard, 12.1(C)
- defined, 35.28
- examples, 35.28(B)
- in hazard, 13.4(A)(3)
- on putting green, 16.1(A)(1), 35.28(B)(1)
- relief, 23.1
- removing generally, 23.1

lost ball
- defined, 35.29
- in abnormal ground condition, 25.2(A)
- in immovable obstruction, 24.3(A)
- in water hazard, 26.1(A)
- procedure, 27.1

marker, See *scorer*

marking and lifting the ball
- generally, See *lifting of ball*
- how to mark and lift, 20.1(B)
- who may mark and lift, 20.1(A)

matches defined
    best-ball, 35.17(E)
    four-ball, 35.17(F)
    foursome, 35.17(C)
    single, 35.17(A)
    three-ball, 35.17(D)
    threesome, 35.17(B)

match play
    ball in motion deflected by player, partner, caddie, or equipment, 19.2(A)
    ball in motion deflected or stopped by opponent, caddie, or equipment, 19.3
    ball moved by opponent in search, 18.3(A)
    ball moved by opponent other than in search, 18.3(B)
    ball moved by player, 18.2
    ball played from wrong place, 20.7(B)
    claims, 2.4
    combining with stroke play prohibited, 33.6(C)
    concession, 2.3
    determining winner, 2.1(B)
    exchanged balls, 15.2(C)
    flagstick, unauthorized attendance, 17.2
    generally, 2
    general penalty, 2.2
    halved hole, 2.1(A)
    information about strokes taken, 2.5
    informing opponent about penalties, 2.5(A)(3)
    making stroke dropped or placed in wrong place, 20.7
    order of play not on teeing ground, 10.1(B)
    order of play on teeing ground, 10.1(A)
    order of play with provisional ball, 10.3
    penalties, See *Appendix 1: Penalty Summary Chart*
    playing from outside teeing ground, 11.4(A)
    playing from wrong teeing ground, 11.5
    practicing before and between rounds, 7.1
    practicing during round, 7.2
    scoring by holes, 2.1(A)
    slow play, 6.7(B)(1), 6.7(C)
    stopping play by agreement, 6.8(A)(3)
    terminology, 2.1(C)
    three-ball match, ball accidentally deflected or stopped by opponent, 30.2(B)
    ties, settling, 2.1(B)
    winner of hole, 2.1(A)

match play (*continued*)
    winner of match, 2.1(B)
    wrong ball, 15.2
maximum number of clubs
    adding and selecting clubs, 4.3(A)
    extra clubs declared out of play, 4.3(D)
    penalty for violating restriction, 4.3(C)
    sharing clubs, 4.3(B)
measuring
    ball moved in, 18.6
    with artificial device, 14.3(A)(2)
medical equipment or devices, 14.3
moved ball, See *ball moved*
multiple strikes of ball, 14.4, 14.5(B)(2)
nearest point of relief
    abnormal ground condition, 25.1(B)
    defined, 35.31
    immovable obstruction, 24.2(B)
    procedures to determine, 35.31(B)
    reference point for re-dropping, 20.2(C)(1)(g)
observer
    as outside agency, 35.36
    defined, 35.32(A)
    restrictions on, 35.32(B)
obstructions
    ball in or on obstruction, 24.1(A)(3)
    ball lost in obstruction, 24.3(A)
    ball not in or on obstruction, 24.1(A)(2)
    Committee declaring movable to be immovable, 35.33(C)
    defined, 35.33
    hindrance with line of play or putt, 24.2(A)
    immovable obstructions, 24.2
    interference from immovable obstruction, 24.2(A)
    in water hazard, 24.2(C)(1)
    movable obstructions, 24.1, 35.33(B)
    relief from generally, 24
    removing in hazard, 13.4(B)(2)(b)
    searching for a ball in, 12.1(E)
    stakes marking ground under repair or water hazard, 35.19(C), 35.52(B)
    touching in hazard, 13.4(B)(6)
    unreasonable situation, 24.2(C)(2)
opponent
    attending flagstick without authority, 17.2
    ball deflected by, 19.3

ball moved by, 18.3
  claims in match play, 2.4
  defined, 35.34
  handicap, 6.2(A)
  late claims in match play, 34.1(A)(2)
  reporting penalty to, 2.5(A)(3)
  three-ball match, 30.2
order of play
  best-ball and four-ball match play, 30.3(B)
  four-ball stroke play, 31.4
  match play, 10.1
  provisional or second ball played from teeing ground, 10.3
  stroke play, 10.2
  threesomes and foursomes, 29.2, 29.3
  when original ball is not played as it lies, 10.1(B)(2),
     10.2(B)(2)
out of bounds
  ball out of play, 35.4(A)
  ball played from water hazard goes out of bounds, 26.2(B)
  Committee's responsibilities, 33.2(A)
  defined, 35.35
  dropped ball rolling out of bounds, 20.2(C)(1)(d)
  markings and margins, 35.35(B)
  objects defining, 13.2(A)(1)(a), 35.33(A)(1), 35.35(B)
  part of ball in bounds, 35.35(C)
  procedure, 27.1
  standing out of bounds, 35.35(C)
outside agency
  ball at rest moved by, 18.1
  defined, 35.36
  deflecting or stopping ball in motion, 19.1
  forecaddie as, 35.16
  purposely deflecting or stopping ball in motion, 19.1(C)
pace of play
  guidelines, 6.7(A)
  preventing slow play, 6.7
  undue delay between holes, 6.7(C)
par competitions, 32.1(A)
partner
  absence in best-ball or four-ball (match play), 30.3(A)
  absence in four-ball (stroke play), 31.2
  defined, 35.37
  included in terms *competitor* and *fellow-competitor*, 35.12(C)
  included in term *you*, 35.37(B)
  indicating your line of play, 8.2(A)

partner (*continued*)
: indicating your line of putt, 8.2(B)
: requesting or giving advice, 8.1
: sharing clubs with, 4.3(B)
: your penalties applying to partner, 30.3(F), 31.8

penalties
: after holing out (match play), 2.2(B)
: canceled when round canceled (stroke play), 33.2(D)
: defined, 35.38
: disqualification penalty: waiving, modifying, or imposing, 33.1(B)
: general penalty (match play), 2.2(A)
: general penalty (stroke play), 3.2(A)
: ignoring by agreement, 1.3
: local rule affecting, 33.1(C)(2)
: refusal to comply with a rule (stroke play), 3.2(B)
: reporting to opponent (match play), 2.5(A)(3)
: reporting to scorer (stroke play), 3.1(B)
: stroke and distance, 27.1(A)
: summary of penalties, See *Appendix 1: Penalty Summary Chart*
: time limit for imposing (match play), 34.1(A)
: time limit for imposing (stroke play), 34.1(B)(2)

penalty stroke, defined, 35.38

Penalty Summary Chart, Appendix 1

placing or returning the ball
: by improper person, 20.3(A)(2)
: by whom, 20.3(A)
: generally, 20.3
: if accidentally moved, 20.3(A)(2)
: lifting ball incorrectly placed, 20.6
: on spot from which it was moved, 20.3(A)(1)
: procedure when play resumed, 6.8(D)
: when ball becomes "in play," 20.4(A)
: when ball won't come to rest on the spot, 20.3(D)
: when original lie is altered, 20.3(C)
: when spot not determinable, 20.3(B)(2)
: where to place, 20.3(B)

player's responsibilities
: caddies, 6.4
: generally, 6
: group, remaining with, 6.3(D)
: handicap, 6.2
: playing continuously, 6.8(A)(1)
: playing the right ball, 6.5

prompt play, 6.7
scoring, 6.6
starting time, 6.3(A)

playing out of turn
    match play, 10.1(C)
    stroke play, 10.2(C)
    stableford competition, 32.2(A)(13)

playing the ball as it lies
    ball in hazard, 13.4
    building a stance, 13.3
    from within a water hazard, 26.2
    generally, 13.1
    improving lie, stance, swing, or line of play, 13.2
    moving ball, 14.5

practice
    after concession, 7.2(C)(2)
    before and between rounds, 7.1
    between holes, 7.2(B)
    Committee may modify practice restrictions, 7.1(C)
    Committee to designate area, 33.2(C)
    generally, 7
    practice putting green, 25.4, 35.54
    restrictions during round, 7.2

practice swing, 7.2(C)(3)

primary rules
    nothing to affect lie of ball, 1.2(B)
    nothing to affect ball in play, 1.2(A)
    penalty for violating, 1.2(D)
    serious violations, 1.2(E)
    specific rule applies, 1.2(C)

procedures
    after playing from wrong place in stroke play, 20.7(C)
    after playing wrong ball
        (match play), 15.2
        (stroke play), 15.3
    claims, 2.4(B)
    determining whether ball is unfit, 5.3(A)
    doubt about (stroke play), 3.4
    dropping ball, 20.2(A)(1)
    identifying ball, 12.2(B)
    lifting ball, 20.1
    nearest point of relief, 35.31(B)
    placing ball after play resumes, 6.8(D)
    provisional ball, 27.2
    reporting to Committee when stopping play, 6.8(A)(2)

procedures (*continued*)
    second ball, 3.4(A)
    unplayable ball, 28.1(B)
protection from the elements, 14.2
provisional ball
    abandoning the provisional ball, 27.2(C)
    becoming the ball in play, 27.2(B)
    conditions for hitting, 27.2(A)(1)
    declaring a provisional ball, 27.2(A)(2)
    defined, 35.39
    failure to abandon, 27.2(C)
    failure to comply, 27.2(A)(3)
    from teeing ground, 10.3
    order of play (match play), 10.3
    order of play (stroke play), 10.3
    original ball lost in water hazard, 27.2(B)(3)
    original ball lost or out of bounds, 27.2(B)(2)
    wrong ball, 35.53(A)(2)
putting green
    abnormal ground condition, 25.1(A)(1), 25.1(B)(3)
    ball lost in abnormal ground condition, 25.2(B)(3)
    ball lost in immovable obstruction, 24.3(C)(3)
    ball moved after touching loose impediment, 23.2(B)
    ball overhanging hole, 16.2
    ball striking flagstick or attendant, 17.3
    ball touching, 35.40(B)
    cleaning ball, 16.1(B), 22.3
    defined, 35.40
    failing to hole out, 3.3
    generally, 16
    indicating line of putt, 8.2(B)
    interference from wrong putting green, 25.4
    lifting ball, 16.1(B)
    line of putt, 8.2(B), 16.1(A)
    loose impediments on, 35.28
    making final-hole claim before leaving final green, 2.4(B)(1)
    nearest point of relief, 24.2(B)(3), 25.1(B)(3)
    no touching line of putt, 16.1(A)
    practice before round, 7.1
    practice between holes, 16.1(D)
    practice during round, 7.2
    redrop situations, 20.2(C)(1)(c)
    relief from abnormal ground condition, 25.1(A)(1), 25.1(B)(3)
    relief from immovable obstruction, 24.2(B)(3)

repairing hole plugs, ball marks, and other damage, 16.1(C)
  testing surface of, 16.1(D)
  wrong putting green, 25.4, 35.54
re-dropping the ball, See *dropping and re-dropping ball*
referee
  as outside agency, 35.36
  Committee's discretion to limit duties, 33.1(A)
  defined, 35.41
  duties, 35.41(A)
  final decisions, 34.2
  match play duties, 35.41(B)
  restrictions, 35.41(C)
relief
  abnormal ground condition, 25.1(B)
  ball lost in abnormal ground condition, 25.2(B)
  ball lost in obstruction, 24.3(B)
  Committee denying relief from abnormal ground condition that affects stance only, 25.1(A)(2)
  Committee restricting relief from obstructions, 24.2(D)(2)
  denying relief when only stance is affected by abnormal ground condition, 25.1(A)(2)
  embedded ball, 25.3(B)
  from immovable obstructions, 24.2(A)
  from movable obstructions, 24.1(A)
  ground under repair, 25.1(B)
  interference from wrong putting green, 25.4(B)
  lateral water hazard, 26.1(B)(2)(c)
  loose impediment, 23.1
  nearest point of, defined, 35.31
  water-hazard options, 26.1(B)
re-placing of ball
  after ball cleaned, 21.2
  after ball lifted for interference, 22.1
  after ball marked and lifted, 20.1
  after ball moved by fellow-competitor, caddie, or equipment (stroke play), 18.4
  after ball moved by outside agency, 18.1
  after ball moved by player, 18.2
  after ball moved by player during address, 18.2
  after ball moved during search, 12.1, 18.3(A)
  after ball moved when loose impediment removed, 23.2
  after ball moves when moving obstruction, 24.1
  after examining for unfitness, 5.3
  after identifying ball, 12.2
  ball moved by another ball, 18.5

re-placing of ball (*continued*)
- ball moved in measuring, 18.6
- by improper person, 20.3(A)(2)
- on putting green, 16.1(B)
- repairing ball marks on putting green, 16.1(C)
- re-placing in wrong place, 20.7
- upon resuming play after suspension, 6.8(D)
- when original lie altered, 20.3(C)
- where to re-place, 20.3(B)
- who can re-place, 20.3

resuming of play after suspension, 6.8(D)

round, stipulated
- defined, 35.46

rub of the green, See *ball deflected by outside agency*, 19.1

rules
- breached in match play (general penalty), 2.2
- breached in stroke play (general penalty), 3.2(A)
- Committee cannot waive rules, 33.1
- defined, 35.42
- disregarding an opponent's violation, 2.4(A)
- ignoring by players' agreement, 1.3
- issues not covered by, 1.4
- local rules, 33.1(C)
- player responsibilities, 6.1
- refusal to comply with a rule (stroke play), 3.2(B)

scorecard
- alteration of (stroke play), 6.6(D)
- recording scores (stroke play), 6.6(A)
- returning scorecard without including an unknown penalty, 6.6(F)
- signing and returning (stroke play), 6.6(B)
- wrong score recorded (stroke play), 6.6(E)

scorer
- as outside agency, 35.36
- defined, 35.43
- disputing claim of unfit ball, 5.3(A)(5)
- examining ball, 5.3(A)(2)
- identifying ball, 12.2(B)
- reporting penalties to, 3.1(B)
- signing scorecard in stroke play, 6.6(A)

scoring
- altering score after return, 6.6(D)
- bogey and par competitions, 32.1(A)(1)
- Committee responsibilities, 33.6(A)
- four-ball stroke play, 31.3

match play, 2.1(A)
player responsibilities, 6.6(B), 6.6(E), 31.3
returning scorecard without including an unknown penalty, 6.6(F)
scorer responsibilities, 6.6(A), 31.3
Stableford, 32.1(B)(1)
stroke play, 3.1, 6.6
wrong score recorded (stroke play), 6.6(E)

searching for and seeing ball
ball covered by sand, 12.1(B)
ball in abnormal ground condition, 12.1(E)
ball in obstruction, 12.1(E)
ball in water hazard, 12.1(D)
ball moved by opponent, caddie, or equipment (match play), 18.3(A)
general rule, 12.1(A)
loose impediments covering ball in hazard, 12.1(C)

second ball
after playing from wrong place, 20.7(C)(2)
as relates to wrong ball, 35.53(A)(3)
determining score for hole, 3.4(B), 20.7(C)(2)(C)
match play, 2.4(B)(3)
order of play, 10.3
played when in doubt about procedure, 3.4(A)
playing from teeing ground, 10.3
reporting to Committee, 3.4(A)

serious violations
correction procedures, 20.7(C)(2)
determining score for hole, 20.7(C)(2)(C)
disqualification, 1.2(E)
intentionally deflecting ball, 19.1(C)
generally, 20.7(C)(1)

side
defined, 35.44
disqualification of in best-ball and four-ball (match play), 30.3(E)
disqualification of in four-ball (stroke play), 31.7
honor on teeing ground, 10.1(A)
order of play in best-ball and four-ball (match play), 30.3(B)
order of play in four-ball (stroke play), 31.4
order of play in threesomes and foursomes, 29.1
representing a side in best ball or four-ball (match play), 30.3(A)
representing a side in four-ball (stroke play), 31.2

side (*continued*)
    violating 14-club rule in best-ball and four-ball (match play), 30.3(D)
    violating 14-club rule in four-ball (stroke play) , 31.6

single
    defined, 35.17(A)

slow play
    generally, 6.7
    penalty, 6.7(B)
    player's responsibilities, 6.7(A)
    undue delay between holes, 6.7(C)

Stableford competitions, 32.1(B)

stance
    abnormal ground condition interfering with, 25.1(A)(1)
    addressing the ball, 35.2
    avoiding interference with tee markers, 11.2
    building, 13.3
    defined, 35.45
    fairly taking, 13.2(B)(1)
    immovable obstruction interfering with, 24.2(A)
    local rule denying relief from interference with, 25.1(A)(2)
    out-of-bounds marker affecting, 35.35(B)
    reasonableness of, in obtaining relief, 24.2(C)(2)(b), 25.1(C)(2)(b)
    restriction on improving stance, 13.2(A)
    standing astride or on line of putt, 16.1(E)
    standing out of bounds, 35.35(C)

starting time
    penalty for tardiness, 6.3(B)
    Committee responsibilities, 6.3, 33.3(A)
    disqualification for tardiness, 6.3(B)
    extraordinary circumstances for tardiness, 6.3(C)
    player's obligation, 6.3(A)

stipulated round
    advice during, 8.1
    caddie rule violations, 6.4(B)
    defined, 35.46
    extending to settle tie, 2.1(B)
    practice during, 7.2
    reducing the number of holes, 33.1(A)

stopping play
    Committee stopping play, 6.8(B)
    generally, 6.8
    player stopping play, 6.8(A)

striking the ball
    artificial devices, 14.4
    fairly, 14.1
    generally, 14
    multiple strikes, 14.5
    no assistance, 14.3
    using clubhead only, 14.1
    while another putted ball is in motion, 16.1(F)
stroke
    advice before playing, 8
    artificial device used in, 14.3
    ball breaking after, 5.4
    canceling for playing out of turn, 10.1(C)
    canceling for putted ball being deflected, 19.1(B)(2)
    conceding, 2.3
    defined, 35.47
    from outside teeing ground, 11.4
    physical assistance during, 14.2
    playing from where previous stroke played, 20.5
    playing from wrong place, 20.7
    striking ball more than once, 14.4
    while another putted ball is in motion, 16.1(F)
    winning hole with fewer strokes (match play), 2.1(A)
    with provisional ball, 27.2
    with wrong ball in best-ball or four-ball (match play), 30.3(C)
    with wrong ball in four-ball (stroke play), 31.5
    with wrong ball in match play, 15.2
    with wrong ball in stroke play, 15.3
stroke and distance, 27.1(B)
stroke play
    agreeing to play out of turn, 10.2(C)
    altering card, 6.6(D)
    ball in motion deflected or stopped by fellow-competitor, caddie, or equipment, 19.4
    ball in motion deflected or stopped by player, caddie, or equipment, 19.2(B)
    ball moved by fellow-competitor, 18.4
    ball moved by player, 18.2
    ball played from outside teeing ground, 11.4(B)
    ball played from wrong place, 20.7
    combining with match play prohibited, 33.6(C)
    determining score with second ball, 3.4(B)
    disqualification, Committee discretion on, 33.1(B)

stroke play (*continued*)
    doubt about procedures, 3.4
    failing to hole out, 3.3
    flagstick, unauthorized attendance, 17.2
    general penalty, 3.2(A)
    groups, changing, 6.3(C)
    groups, Committee to arrange, 33.3(A)
    handicap, 6.2(C)
    informing scorer about penalties, 3.1(B)
    new holes, 33.2(B)(I)
    order of play on teeing ground, 10.2(A)
    order of play with provisional ball, 10.3
    penalties, generally, 1.2(D), 3.1(B), 3.2
    penalties, reporting to scorer, 3.1(B)
    penalties, time limit for imposing, 34.1(B)
    penalty, caddie violations, 6.4(E)
    penalty, failing to start on time, 6.3
    penalty, 14-club maximum, 4.3(C)
    playing from outside teeing ground, 11.4(B)
    playing next stroke from where previous stroke played, 20.5
    playing out of turn, 10.2(C)
    playing stroke after dropping or placing ball in wrong place, 20.7(C)
    practicing before and between rounds, 7.1(B)
    recording scores, 6.6(A)
    refusal to comply with a rule, 3.2(B)
    scoring, 3.1, 6.6, 33.6(A)
    second-ball procedures, 3.4
    signing and returning card, 6.6(B)
    slow play, 6.7(B), (C)
    winning at, 3.1(A)
    wrong ball, 15.3
    wrong score recorded, 6.6(E)
substituted ball
    abnormal ground condition, 25.1(D)(I)
    as relates to ball in play, 35.4(B)
    as relates to lost ball, 35.29(B)
    defined, 35.48
    generally, 15.1(A)
    improper substitution, 15.1(B)
    improper substitution when playing from wrong place, 20.7
    improper substitution when returning your ball to play, 20.3
    lifting ball incorrectly substituted, 20.6

original ball not recoverable, 18.7(A), 19.1(A)
 relief from obstruction, 24.1(C)(I), 24.2(D)(I)
 when in play, 20.4
suspension of play
 by Committee, 6.8(B), 33.2(D)
 practice during, 7.3
 procedure for players, 6.8(D)
swing
 interference, abnormal ground condition, 25.1(A)
 interference, tee markers, 11.2
 interference, obstruction, 24.2(A)
 interference, wrong putting green, 25.4(A)
 nearest point of relief, 35.31(B)
 practice, 7.2(C)(3)
 reasonableness of, in obtaining relief, 24.2(C)(2)(b), 25.1(C)(2)(b)
 stroke, See *stroke*
team competitions, indicating line of putt, advice, 8.3
tee
 defined, 35.49
 nonconforming tee, 11.1
 teeing ball, 11.1
teeing ground
 ball falling off tee, 11.3
 ball inside, 35.50(B)
 defined, 35.50
 order of play (match play), 10.1(A)
 order of play (stroke play), 10.2(A)
 order of play (threesome or foursome), 29.1
 playing from outside, 11.4, 20.7
 playing from the wrong one, 11.5, 20.7
 practice on or near before rounds, 7.1(B)
 practice on or near during round, 7.2(B)
 previous stroke played from, 20.5(A)(1)
 provisional or second ball, 10.3
 standing outside to play ball within, 11.1
 teeing the ball, 11.1
 tee-markers, 11.2
 time limit for match play claims, 2.4(B)(I)
 wrong teeing ground, 11.5
tee-markers
 defining teeing ground, 35.50(A)
 generally, 11.2
testing of conditions
 before stroke play, 7.1(B)(I)

testing of conditions (*continued*)
    in hazard, 13.4
    on putting green, 16.1(D)

three-ball match play, 30.2
    ball at rest moved by an opponent, 30.2(A)
    ball deflected or stopped by an opponent, 30.2(B)
    defined, 35.17(D)
    Rules of Golf apply, 30.1

threesomes
    defined, 35.17(B)
    general format, 29.1
    incorrect order (match play), 29.2
    incorrect order (stroke play), 29.3

through the green
    abnormal ground condition, 25.1(B)(1)
    ball lost in abnormal ground condition, 25.2(B)(1)
    ball lost in immovable obstruction, 24.3(C)(1)
    ball moved after player touches loose impediment, 23.2(A)
    defined, 35.51
    embedded ball, 25.3
    improving lie of ball, etc., 13.2
    previous stroke played from , 20.5(A)(2)
    relief from immovable obstruction, 24.2(B)(1)

ties
    Committee responsibilities, 33.5
    extending stipulated round to settle (match play), 2.1(B)

touching ball
    by opponent, 18.3
    by player, 18.2
    purposely touching or deflecting ball, 1.2

unplayable ball
    bunker restriction, 28.2
    cleaning ball, 28.1(C)
    declaring a ball unplayable, 28.1(A)
    generally, 28
    procedures, 28.1(B)

unplayable course, generally, 33.2(D)

violating a specific rule, 1.2(C)

water hazard
    as relates to provisional ball, 27.2(C)(2)
    ball in, 26
    ball lost in abnormal ground condition, 25.2(B)(4)
    ball lost in obstruction, 24.3(C)(4)
    ball moving in, 14.6, 26.1(D)

ball played within becomes lost or unplayable outside
    hazard, 26.2(B)
ball played within comes to rest in same hazard, 26.2(A)
ball touching, 35.52(C)
casual water, 35.8(A)
cleaning ball after lifting, 26.1(C)
defined, 35.52
lateral water hazard, See *lateral water hazard*
markings and margins, 35.52(B)
no relief from abnormal ground condition, 25.1(C)(1)
no relief from immovable obstructions, 24.2(C)
playing moving ball in, 14.5(B)(3), 14.6
probing in during search, 12.1(D)
relief options, 26.1(B)
searching for ball in, 12.1(D)
wear and alteration of clubs, generally, 4.1(D)
wrong ball
    as relates to provisional ball, 27.2(C)(2)
    correcting mistake (stroke play), 15.3(C)
    defined, 35.53
    exchanged balls (match play), 15.2(C)
    four-ball (match play), 30.3(C)
    four-ball (stroke play), 31.5
    generally, 15.1(A)
    penalty (match play), 15.2(A)
    penalty (stroke play), 15.3(A)
    strokes with (match play), 15.2
    strokes with (stroke play), 15.3
    time spent playing, 35.29(A)
wrong information about strokes (match play), 2.5
wrong place
    ball played from (match play), 20.7(B)
    ball played from (stroke play), 20.7(C)
    generally, 20.7(A)
    lifting ball dropped or placed at, 20.6
    serious violations in stroke play, 20.7(C)(2)(a)
wrong putting green
    defined, 35.54
    interference from, 25.4(A)
    relief procedures, 25.4(B)
wrong score for hole, 6.6(E)

JEFFREY S. KUHN is a lawyer and a volunteer USGA rules official. He has achieved the highest rating at PGA/USGA rules workshops and has officiated at US Opens, US Amateurs, and numerous other USGA championships.

BRYAN A. GARNER is the author of several best-selling books, including *Garner's Modern American Usage*, *Legal Writing in Plain English*, and *The Chicago Guide to Grammar, Usage, and Punctuation*, the latter two published by the University of Chicago Press. He is also editor-in-chief of *Black's Law Dictionary*.